THE
ROYAL HOSPITAL SCHOOL, GREENWICH

The Royal Hospital School, Greenwich

by

H. D. T. Turner

PHILLIMORE

1980

Published by
PHILLIMORE & CO. LTD.
London and Chichester

Head Office: Shopwyke Hall,
Chichester, Sussex, England

ISBN 0 85033 372 5

Printed in Great Britain by
GARDEN CITY PRESS LTD.
Letchworth, Herts.

CONTENTS

LIST OF ILLUSTRATIONS

Plates

(between pages 20 and 21)

(between pages 52 and 53)

(*between pages 116 and 117*)

Figures

FOREWORD

The true 'bones' of History are original sources and this book is a rare miscellany of the life and times of a Royal Hospital School boy during the twenties. Just occasionally the thread of history through to the present day appears—perhaps in a name long forgotten but still on a board here in the School, or in a piece of slang used regularly by present day boys.

Life was very different, and it is vividly and sympathetically illuminated by an author with an excellent memory and a keen eye.

Boys at Holbrook in the future will be able to dip into the School's past with an intimacy never before possible and both we, and our successors, are in the author's debt.

N. B. WORSWICK
March 1980

To all boys
of the Royal Hospital School,
past, present and future

PREFACE

I have been back several times to visit the old school since I left in 1930. It is now the National Maritime Museum, but in my days there it was Greenwich Royal Hospital School. My first visit was in 1957, and as I sat at table in the restaurant,* I compared its snow-white linen, sparkling glassware, gleaming cutlery, and smartly dressed waitresses with the kitchen that I knew with its massive ovens, steaming coppers, and white-aproned, clog-footed cooks.

Since then I have from time to time considered writing of the life, routine with its rigid discipline, peculiar language and customs, and to describe some of the personalities who were there. On a visit in 1964, which lasted several days, I had opportunity not only to visit the museum, but also the many antique and book shops which abound in the town. To my enquiries, there appeared to be little knowledge of the school, and no record of the ship which was built on the parade ground.

I sat on one of the seats on the Colonnade, and looked at the buildings which now seemed so quiet, like some old church or castle silently brooding on its history. The grass-covered parade ground seemed to add to the tranquillity. I thought of the thousands of boys who had lived and trained there, and had contributed so much to the Navy and to the Country during the school's varied existence in the past two and a half centuries, and I decided that I would record my experience there from 1926 until 1930 to fill this gap.

The autobiography and vocabulary is almost entirely from memory, although, fortunately, I kept a diary during 1929 while at the school from which I based the chapters dealing

*I believe at the time it was being used to augment the catering arrangements at the college.

with that period. Since completing the original manuscript, photographs and other material have been obtained. These have not only helped to confirm parts of my story, but also to increase the scope of the work.

Historical facts and records of the school are few and difficult to find; however, after a lot of research I have gathered the information recorded in the three chapters headed Part One of this book.

ACKNOWLEDGMENTS

I would like to acknowledge the help of the following:

The Local History Library, Greenwich; the National Maritime Museum, London; D.O.E., Greenwich Park, London; Capt. L. H. Oliphant, D.S.C., R.N., Ret.; A. Gibson; Old Boys of Greenwich R. H. School and Boreman Boys; Members of the Royal Hospital School Old Boys' Association, especially Lt. C. W. Hall, R.N., Ret. (Vice President), without whose help this book would not have been published.

Finally, many thanks to my wife and son, Raymond, for their moral and practical support during the number of years taken to produce this work.

The illustration on the half title page is the figurehead on the first Fame *(see page 26) and that on the title page is of the figurehead of the second* Fame *in its present position at Holbrook.*

PART ONE

Chapter One

HISTORY OF THE SCHOOL

FOLLOWING THE BATTLE OF LA HOGUE, when the French Fleet was destroyed and the invasion transports burned in 1692, a Charter dated 25 October 1694 was drawn up by William and Mary. It provided for:

(1) The relief and support of seamen serving aboard the ships and vessels belonging to the Navy Royal of Us, Our Heirs and Successors, or employed in Our or Their service at sea, who by reason of age, wounds or other disabilities shall be incapable of further service at sea and be unable to maintain themselves;

(2) The sustentation of the widows of seamen happening to be slain or disabled in such sea service;

(3) The maintenance and education of the children of seamen happening to be slain or disabled in such sea service;

(4) The further relief and encouragement of seamen;

(5) The improvement of navigation;

and decreed that new Greenwich Palace begun by Charles II should now be completed and devoted to the care of disabled seamen.

This was the ruin of the Palace of Placentia which had been a royal residence since 1428, birthplace of Henry VIII, and favourite residence of the Tudors and since had fallen into decay. Charles, who first began rebuilding on the ruins by starting the construction of the King's House, had let the scheme lapse. It was this site that was chosen by the queen. Sir Christopher Wren furnished gratuitously the plans, and the building commenced.

Mary died shortly afterwards, and the work at Greenwich became William's chief preoccupation, partly it is felt for the original reasons, and partly as a memorial to Mary. The building progressed during Anne's reign, until accommodation was

1

available in 1704, and the first 42 occupants arrived in June 1705.

Almost fifty years later, in 1752, the chapel and Queen Mary building were completed, and the hospital was almost finished. After 1705 the number of applications rose as quickly as the hospital places became available. By the end of 1755 there were already one thousand five hundred and fifty. But it was not before another 60 years had elapsed that the buildings were completed and the maximum 2,710 housed. This number was maintained without much variation until 1849 when the numbers declined, mainly due to the deaths of the survivors of the old war, the long peace that followed it, and the granting of a large number of out-pensions, until by 1865 the in-pensioners numbered only 1,420, the vacancies being one thousand, three hundred and ten. In this year an Act was passed to induce the in-pensioners to accept a Greenwich Hospital pension in lieu of board and lodging, and so the hospital was finally closed as such in 1869 to become, eventually, the college and Dreadnought hospital as we know it today.

Under the original foundation of 1694, a school for the sons of seamen so killed in action had been envisaged as forming part of the hospital. This was implemented in 1712 when the first boys arrived. They were assembled in that block of buildings nearest Greenwich pier and known as the King's House, and clothed in uniforms similar to that of the pensioners. The cost of their maintenance and education was partly borne by showing visitors around the Painted Hall and from the sale of old stores.

It was not until 1715 that arrangements were made for 10 of the boys to attend the school of Mr. Thomas Weston, to be instructed in a curriculum that included 'the Italian method of book-keeping, mathematics in three languages, drawing, fencing, music as well as a wide variety of languages and navigation'.

Weston, who was Assistant Astronomer Royal and a specialist in the art of navigation which, as at the similar institution of the Royal Mathematical School at Christ's Hospital, was to be the principle object of study. Weston's portrait appears on the ceiling of the Painted Hall and he charged an entrance fee to visitors to the Hall.

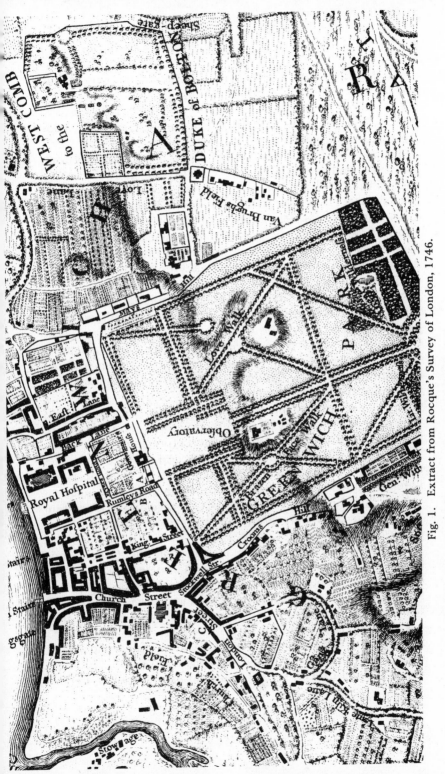

Fig. 1.   Extract from Rocque's Survey of London, 1746.

A Weston's Academy, 1712; B Burney's Academy, 1758; C Greencoat Collegiate, 1672.

At that time John Flamstead was the Astronomer Royal, and he wrote of his assistant as 'An ingenious but sickly youth', but to be fair to Thomas Weston, only once is he referred to as 'sickly', and on many occasions favourable references are made regarding his ingenuity.

Thomas Weston's school went by the name of Weston's Academy, and it stood on the eastern side at the southern end of King William Street, Greenwich, and a few yards from the entrance to Greenwich Park. Like other schools in the district it owed its inspiration to St. Alphage church. It is not known how many pupils were receiving education at Weston's, which was a fee-paying school, other than the boys from the hospital, but it was patronised by many of the leading families of Greenwich (see Fig. 1).

Some information about the academy may be gleaned from the newspapers of the time, as a cutting from one shows that a public acting of plays was a part of the education there. 'The Ingenious Mr Weston of Greenwich having lately erected a theatre for the use and diversion of the young gentlemen under his tuition, the play Marlowe's "Tamberlaine" was last week performed there with vast applause.'

A further notice appears under the date 14 April 1722: 'This day the scholers of Mr. Weston of Greenwich are to perform the tragedy of Tamberlaine before the Lords of the Admiralty . . .'. The mention of the Admiralty emphasises the intimate connection between the academy and the Navy. Later on, however, the education became more professional.

The first Greenwich Hospital school regulations date from 1719 when they were drawn up by the directors and later confirmed by a General Court.

By 1731, 60 boys were in residence in the Queen Anne block of the hospital. The rules state that on leaving school the boys are 'To be put out as Apprentices to Masters of ships and substantial Commanders, for better improvements of their talents, and becoming Able Seaman and good Artists' (i.e., navigators). The school thus provided most of the master's mates in the Royal Navy. When such a mate rose to the post of master or principle navigator, he might go on to become a commissioned officer, so that many hospital schoolboys ended their careers as captains or admirals. (It has been said that by Nelson's day half the flag-officers in the fleet had received their instruction at Weston's Academy.) Two of them of some importance were James Wolfe (General Wolfe of Quebec), and Jack Jervis (Admiral Earl St. Vincent). The latter was at Quebec with his schoolfriend, and was entrusted by Wolfe with his last message home and the jewelled portrait of his fiancée. They both lived at Greenwich, near to where the railway station now stands. They were, of course, fee-paying pupils, so their relationship to the Royal Hospital boys could be described as Old Boys once removed.

In order to enter the school a boy had to be between the ages of 11 and 13, sound in body and in mind, able to read, the son of a seaman or pensioner, and willing to 'conform to the Rules of the School and to behave himself in all respects as he ought'. It was also laid down that 'each boy shall have an everyday Jacket and a serge Waistcoat, made out of the Pensioner's old clothes, and an Irish Ram Skin pair of Breeches once in two years. Each boy shall have a clean shirt, neck and a pair of hose once a week; pillow case once a month; towel as often as necessary'.

Some idea of the quality of the teaching and the disposal of the hospital boys may be gathered from the following list of articles which a J. Cook took with him when apprenticed to a ship in 1743:

3 Cotton Shirts, chequered.	1 Flock Bed.
2 White do. do.	1 Pr. Blankets.
1 Double breasted Pea Jacket.	1 Rug.
1 Course do. do. do.	1 Flock Pillow.
1 Lined Serge Waistcoat.	1 Pillow Case.
1 Blue Jersey do.	1 Navigation Book.
1 Pr. Fine Cloth Breeches.	1 Mathematics Book.
1 Pr. Shag do. do.	1 Writing do.
1 dougett Suit of Clothes.	1 Spelling do.
3 Silk Handkerchiefs.	1 New Testament
2 Prs. Yarn Hose.	1 Atkinson Epitome.
1 Pr. Worsted Hose.	1 Gunter's Scale.
2 Prs. Shoes.	1 Great Pr of Compasses.
1 Hat.	1 Sector.
1 Worsted Cap.	1 Case of Instruments.
1 Chest, Hasp & Padlock.	1 Slate & Pencil.

In 1747 the number of boys rose to 100, and the Commissioners decided that the hospital had to have a school building of its own. The new building was erected on the site of Weston's Academy, which had moved to a building some three hundred yards to the west, where it was known as Burney's Academy, and some time later the area became known as Burney Street. On completion of the buildings in 1758 the 35 years' association of attending the Weston-Burney school as day boys came to an end. Now the boys continued to sleep in Queen Anne's Building, to take meals in the room beneath the Painted Hall, and attend the new school daily.

In 1756 a peaked leather cap was adopted and remained part of the school uniform for over a century. For years the boys were taunted by the town boys with:

> Three pieces of leather, sewn together,
> Makes a Hospital boy's cap

Their diet included two pints of beer a day. The first sports equipment was issued in 1766 because it was found that the boys were liable to play truant unless furnished with 'bats and balls and other articals of like nature'.

The number of boys continued to increase over the next 25 years, and it was recommended in 1783 that a larger school be built on the same site. This would include a dormitory for the boys, and the rooms they had occupied in the hospital 'could be converted to wards for the reception of the Pensioners'. Accordingly a building designed by Mr. Stuart, the late surveyor, under the supervision of Mr. Newton, Clerk of Works, was erected on the site of the old burial ground. It was 146ft. in length, and 42ft. in breadth. On the ground floor was a schoolroom 100ft. long capable of containing 200 boys. On the two floors above were dormitories of the same size fitted with hammocks for the boys to sleep in. Adjoining were rooms for the guardian nurses and other necessary attendants, and at a small distance, a good house for the schoolmaster. It continued as a self-contained Royal Hospital school until 1821 when it was incorporated into the new school as the infirmary (see plates 1 and 37).

Chapter Two

THE BRITISH ENDEAVOUR (SCHOOL)

FOLLOWING THE 1797 mutinies and the decline of the Press Gang, the need for naval recruiting to receive some impetus led to the establishment of a more ambitious school to be run on the lines of its military counterpart, the Duke of York School. In 1798 a Mr. Thompson founded at Paddington a charity school for younger children which he called The British Endeavour, which accommodated about seventy children. This received official support (Lord Nelson was a member of the Committee), and royal patronage.

In 1805 George III resolved to make this a Royal Foundation for 1,000 children, and following Nelson's famous victories, when public feeling ran high, large sums were raised. In 1806 on 21 October, the first anniversary of the Battle of Trafalgar, it was moved to the Queen's House at Greenwich, where it was re-named The Royal Asylum.

To accommodate the then 700 boys and girls, two large wings with connecting colonnades were built, being completed in 1807. This school may be considered as a junior school with only a few of the more clever children being elevated to the senior hospital school, still being housed in the building designed by Stuart in King William Street, and what was later used as the infirmary. The discipline was harsh, and the younger children merely taught to read and write.

In 1821 it was considered uneconomical to have two similar schools so near to each other to exist as separate foundations, so they were amalgamated under the name of 'The Naval Asylum'. By 1825, however, it was decided 'that the title of Asylum now be discontinued and that the schools be henceforth designated as the Upper and Lower Schools of the "Royal Hospital" '; hence the name 'Royal Hospital Schools' came into

KEY

283c   Roan School
457, 461   Burney
273   Site of Dr. Weston's
         School

Fig. 2. Map of Greenwich, 1844

use, but were officially called Greenwich Hospital Schools, until 1892 when 'Royal Hospital School' was adopted.

Although there was a captain superintendent and a head-master for the whole establishment, the schools continued to be run separately on account of the nature of the curriculum and the regulations controlling the mode of entry. In 1825 the numbers were:

Boys, Upper School	200
Boys, Lower School	600
Girls, Lower School	200
Total	1,000

Boys entering the Upper School at the age of 11 or 12 were nominated by the Admiralty, the Commissioners of Greenwich Hospital, Lloyd's Patriotic Fund Committee or certain ship-owners. They remained at school for three years before joining the Navy as master's mates, or the Merchant Service. Those entering the Lower School underwent no education tests and left at the age of fourteen. At one period the Upper School was further sub-divided to include a Nautical Division, a kind of sixth form.

On 25 August 1821 Mr. Edward Riddle was selected as Master of the old Greenwich School, the Upper School. He left Trinity House school, Newcastle, to take the appointment.

He had already published his book on navigation, and *Riddle's Navigation* was the text-book for the Navy and Merchant Service for over fifty years. As an observer he was unsurpassed.

There were three points to which he specially turned his attention:

(1) The theoretical proof of every rule.
(2) Chart drawings.
(3) Observing.

With this training many of the boys who entered the Navy as master's assistants were perfect masters of the subjects of Navigation and Nautical Astronomy, and many became distinguished in their profession.

Nearly all the officers of the Hydrographic Department of the Admiralty (at one time there were but two exceptions) were his pupils. Captain Robert C. Allen, C.B., famous for his service in the Arctic regions, and Mr. G. F. McDougall, the accomplished surveyor and artist, and author of *The Voyage of the Resolute,* were two of his first pupils.

Edward Riddle was Master of the Upper School until 1851, when he was succeeded by his son, Mr. John Riddle. A bust of both stood for many years in the hall of the Queen's House.

The girls' school was not a success. It was decided in 1841 to close it; the girls were sent home, with an allowance of £12 per year, to be paid during the time that they would otherwise have remained at the school, on condition that they attended some school in their neighbourhood and were supervised by a parent or friends.

Some years later it was reported that the girl monitors had not been a success; they lived with the other girls and were able to exert very little influence over them. They had applied for separate cabins, such as that occupied by Diana Harris, a blind girl who had been appointed school organist. She lost her sight while at the school, and was sent to the 'Indigent Blind School' at St. George's Fields, where she learned to play the organ, and in 1829 returned to the school and was appointed to play the organ in the chapel which was then in part of the West Wing (see plate 4).

After 1828 sons of officers were accepted in the Upper School, but the Lower School remained open only to the sons of seamen not above the rank of Warrant Officer. The sons of merchant seamen continued to be admitted as they had been during the previous century. The reputation of the Upper School remained high throughout the century chiefly because of the inspired teaching of Edward Riddle.

The school was inspected in 1844 on behalf of the committee of the Privy Council on Education and a sorry state of affairs was revealed. It was found that half the boys could not read (which was hardly surprising when we know that two masters were in charge of 600 boys), and that many of the younger boys spent most of their time making clothes and shoes for the rest of the school. An increase in staff was made and 16 pupil teachers from the senior school were employed; but when geometry was introduced into the syllabus of the Lower School 42 boys ran away. The school was now reorganised into the Lower School of 387 boys, entering at the age of nine, an Upper School of 210, entering at 12 and leaving at 15, and a Nautical Division of 171, entering at 12 and leaving at fifteen. The total was seven hundred and sixty-eight. It was at this time that the first 'Ship' was erected on the parade ground.

Over the years the Hospital Estate had acquired additional areas of land. By 1810 the sites on which stood Weston's Academy and the Grey Coat school (Roan school) had been added, and on the latter site the Dreadnought hospital was later built.

Since the school's foundation, three burial grounds had been procured; the first was at the foot of Maze Hill in the north-east corner of the park. This site was later used for the hospital's first infirmary, then as the residential apartments for the masters of the hospital school, and eventually as private residences.

The second burial ground was at the corner of Romney Road and King William Street (where Stuart's new school was built), and is now the site of Davenport House.

In the late 1860s about three thousand bodies (mostly pensioners from the hospital) were removed from this cemetery and were re-buried in a third ground about one mile to the east at the corner of Woolwich Road and Chevening Road, East Greenwich.

I read an undated record: 'The burial ground is still tidy and open to visitors, and the names of the boys who are buried there are still distinguishable upon the stones'. In 1978 it was being used as a small park kept by the London Borough of Greenwich Leisure Services.

In 1977 an Old Boy wrote: 'Some weeks ago before the end of the Summer Holidays I paid one of my regular visits to the Maritime Museum as I am fortunate enough to be living nearby. Although I am not a Greenwich Schoolboy and my main ties lie with Holbrook, I still have very nostalgic memories of Greenwich. I can remember my parents often taking me past the School in one of the old London trams and seeing all the young boys in their uniforms in the grounds and still quite clearly remember the *Fame.*

'If one leaves the Museum and proceeds down the main road in the direction of Woolwich, past Blackwall Lane, you will come to a small park which is now known as East Greenwich Pleasance. This was originally the Royal Navy Cemetery and has very long connections with both the School and the Naval College. The original main entrance with its old Victorian buildings is now closed as the council have built a Children's Welfare Clinic behind it. But if you turn into Chevening Road at the side, the entrance is about 100 yards up on the right. On the original side wall, let into the brickwork is a small stone plaque with the inscription "GREENWICH HOSPITAL 1857", so I assume that this was when the Cemetery opened.

'Upon entering the Pleasance, which I estimate to be 8 to 10 acres, is a large stone tablet on the wall with the following inscription:

OPPOSITE THIS TABLET LIE INTERRED THE REMAINS
OF ABOUT 3,000 MEN FORMERLY PENSIONERS OF THE
ROYAL HOSPITAL REMOVED FROM THE INFIRMARY
BURYING GROUND IN 1875.

THEY SERVED THEIR COUNTRY IN THE WARS WHICH
ESTABLISHED THE NAVAL SUPREMACY OF ENGLAND
AND DIED, THE HONOURED RECIPIENTS OF HER
GRATITUDE.

'Most of this site is now laid out as a park with lawns and very nice flower beds, but there are still about 200 graves and head-stones remaining in four separate little groups. The most impressive of these is one with a full size anchor on the grave and is of a Rear Admiral who was President of the Royal Naval College. The most interesting grave is Captain Edmund Cooper-Key's grave; he was Captain Superintendent of the School from 1906 to 1922. He died in 1933. His father was the first President of the Royal Naval College, Greenwich and was Vice-Admiral Sir Astley Cooper-Key. Other members of the School staff buried there include Lieut. Commander S. T. P. Yeo, who was Chief Officer of the School from 1925 to 1933, and

Captain Charles Burney who was Superintendent of the School from 1870 until 1887.

'The following graves of instructors who are buried with their wives include Henry Williams who was at the School for 21 years and died in 1903 aged 59; Arthur Daniels who was at the School for 22 years died 1904 aged 51; James Spencer 22 years at the School died 1904; Alfred Randall who died in 1908 aged 63 years and Walter Maby who was at the School for 20 years and died in 1929 aged 65 years. Other graves include two Headmasters, Albert Escott F.R.A.S. who died in 1891 aged 51 and George Pulsford F.R.A.S. who died 1899.

'There are a few graves of young boys between the ages of 12 and 16 but only one that actually states he was a Royal Hospital Schoolboy. This is Owen Sexton who died in 1932 aged 15.

'There is also the grave of Benjamin Bevans who was for 20 years Verger and Yeoman of Greenwich Royal Hospital Chapel and died in 1927 aged 84 years. Further interesting headstones include Thomas Joseph Mott, Crimean veteran who died in 1913 aged 72 years and was Seamanship Instructor to King George Vth. Sir John Liddell K.C.B. M.C. F.R.S. Main Director of the Medical Department of the Royal Navy who died in 1868. John Davidson M.D.C.B. Inspector General R.N. who died in January 1881 aged 64 years. Two veterans of Trafalgar—Captain Henry Parker R.N. who was a midshipman on the *Belleisle* at Trafalgar who died in 1873 aged 84 years and Captain Mark Halpen Sweny who served on *Colossus.*

'One thing I noticed were the graves of quite a few casualties of the First World War, which seemed to be regularly attended to and all had white and mauve flower beds on them. There were also a few graves of Army Captains/Colonels.

'Many of the older headstones are no longer readable and it is very sad to see that vandals have damaged the headstones.

'On my way out I met one of the Park keepers who I worked with over 20 years ago, and after a lengthy conversation, I bade him farewell and asked him to keep an eye on all the Old Boys and Staff resting there.'

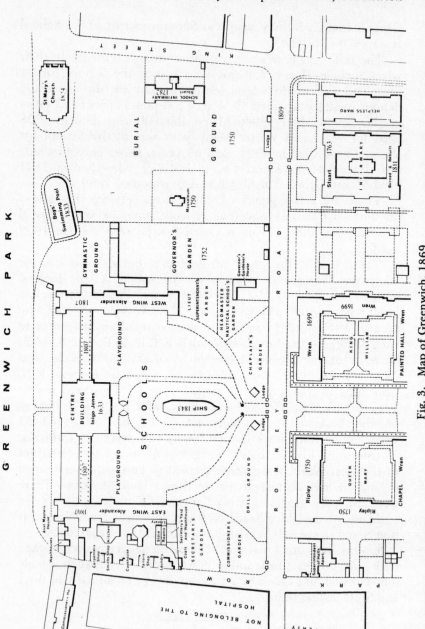

Fig. 3. Map of Greenwich, 1869.

I find that in 1859 'the two schools were separated by an oval, walled-in ground extending from the terrace of the Queen's House to near the gates. At that time there were two schools, the Upper School for the sons of Officers of the Royal Navy and Royal Marines, and a Lower School for the sons of ratings'. A writer, a member of the Upper School, describes his uniform as 'a pea jacket, waistcoat trousers and glengarry cap, an ordinary white shirt with a soft turned down collar fastened at the throat with a black ribbon tied in a bow knot'.

Another writer, 1860–66, describes his uniform as 'a cloth Pea Jacket in summer and a double breasted Reefer in winter with the usual brass buttons. There were eight companies of one hundred, each having four sections, with a Captain to each section and a Head Captain over all. These Captains were distinguished by a badge worn on the arm on which a crown and anchor was worked in white'.

During this period the acceptance of sons of officers was discontinued, there now being a common entry for all at the same level and with the same opportunities. The qualification for the Upper School was now through educational examination, the successful boys passing across the ground to what was now the Nautical School. The dining hall was then at the extreme end of this (east) wing (see plate 2).

The daily routine in 1863 commenced with the boys being roused by the officer in charge walking through the dormitories ringing a large bell. Beds were made, and after prayers a rush to the washing lavatories. Breakfast was at eight o'clock until half past, followed by classes at nine o'clock. From twelve until twelve forty-five it was drill, and at one o'clock it was 'Fall in for dinner'. The band would take up their station near the railings, and at a quick march the boys would march past the gun, on to the dining hall situated at the end of the school. If it was raining, it was 'Fall in' under the colonnade, down under the Queen's House (The Subway), and up the other side.

Classes followed from two until five. Tea at six o'clock and to bed at eight.

The drill for the first-year boys was marching, forming fours, etc. The second year, single stick and cutlass. Third year, gun drill on board *Fame*, and lastly, going aloft furling sails, etc. In 1863 this would have been on board the new *Fame,* or the second ship.

For gymnastics a trench about three feet deep and one hundred yards long was made. Into this was laid long faggots of wood, and all filled in with tan (spent bark from tan pits), to prevent accidents when falling. At each end was a pole about a foot in diameter, surmounted by an iron cross arrangement. One cross had four long ropes for giant strides; the other was simply for climbing. There were also parallel bars and horizontal bars. These were all used in the open in all weathers.

During 1864 the extension to the school observatory was built, including the third observation dome.

In 1867 the routine was, in summer, up at 5 a.m. and off to the swimming bath, breakfast at eight, review of boys at 8.30 by the head, and at 9 o'clock into class until 12 o'clock. Drill by companies until 12.45 p.m., when all formed up and were marched to the dining hall.

Dinner was finished at 1.30 p.m., and it was free time until 2 o'clock, when it was again classes until 4.30 p.m. At 5 o'clock it was tea-time, and after until 7 o'clock it was free time. Classes again until 8 p.m., when they were all marched off to bed.

Meals were as follows: breakfast—a jam-jar of cocoa, bread and butter on four days, bread and dripping on three; dinner during the summer—four days roast beef and potatoes, and the other three days roast mutton; in winter—Monday, roast beef; Tuesday, boiled beef and macaroni soup; Wednesday, roast beef; Thursday, mutton; Friday, beef; Saturday, boiled pork and pea soup; Sunday, roast beef and duff. Tea: as breakfast but butter every day.

On Saturdays the boys were allowed out in town from 2 p.m. to 5 p.m. On Sundays those who had relatives near were allowed out until 7 p.m. Pupil teachers' food was the same as the boys, except the duff on Sundays had currants in it.

When Captain Burney took over the school in 1870 he had the dress of the boys changed, but not of the pupil teachers. The boys now had navy uniforms with white straw hats. Instead of attending classes each day, the system of one day classes, one day 'trades' (having to work in various 'shops'—tailors, shoemakers, sail, carpenters, kitchen, laundry, etc.), was started at this time.

During Captain Burney's time discipline was tightened up; there were public floggings nearly every day. Leave on Saturday afternoons was stopped; instead the boys were employed washing and scrubbing out the dormitories, dining-hall and classrooms. The writer quotes, 'It was different during Rev. Holmes' time, he treated us like gentlemen, but Burney's OH!!!' The pupil teachers, who had previously slept in the Queen's House, were turned out and had to sleep, one to each dormitory, on a raised stand so as to overlook the boys.

The Greenwich hospital closed in 1869 and the control of the school was transferred to the Board of Admiralty. Its curriculum and organisation were examined by various committees set up by the Board, and their findings were far from satisfactory. It was found that the teaching was too academic for the boys at the Lower School, so more emphasis was laid on learning a trade. It was also found that the diet had been much reduced in the interests of economy and that the physical development of the boys had been affected.

The third and last 'ship' *Fame* was built during 1872 and the school was now beginning to take on the familiar appearance as we now know it. During 1877 and 1884 the gymnasium and the new west wing and dining-room wing were built. These were not on the map published in 1877, but appeared on the General Plan of Greenwich Hospital Estate 1884.

An 'Old Boy' writes, 'I well remember 14th March 1877, when at the age of thirteen I entered the School. The first building I entered was the Gym. and when I looked into it, it was nearly empty. How I opened my eyes to see its size and the big stage at the far end; I had never seen such a big building'.

In 1880 there was a headmaster, three masters, one in charge of each section of the school; the remainder were senior and junior pupil teachers. The school pioneered the use of pupil teachers in the late 18th century, for the system of employing such boys was not established in Britain until many years later. A Mr. Lancy was not only the first pupil teacher, but is reputed to be the first Royal Hospital schoolboy to become the headmaster at the school, in 1800. He took the vacancy when Thomas

Furber resigned the headmastership on account of failing eyesight, and started with the salary of £250 a year, from which sum he paid the salaries to his then three assistant teachers, one of whom was a Mr. Boyd who was also a boy at the school.

An interesting fact is that during this period it became quite a teachers' training school. About fifty teachers in Greenwich, Deptford, Woolwich and Poplar, including the Roan School and Goldsmiths, were Royal Hospital School Old Boys who had been trained as masters' assistants and had graduated upwards. Some were employed as far distant as Portsmouth polytechnic. It is thought that the prefix P.D. for master, is a derivation of P.T. (pupil teacher), which appears more likely than 'Punishment Deliverer' which I was taught it meant when I was at the school, however apt the latter may seem.

At the bi-centenary of the school in 1894 it is a good time to pause and look back over the previous 60 years. Subtle changes had taken place. Slates and chalk in the classrooms were superseded by paper and quill, the boys being taught how to cut a pen from a feather. Later the quills were replaced by steel-nibbed pens. Piped water was laid on, prior to which the transport of water for the pensioners as well as the boys and staff at the school was from the well in Greenwich Park, which is still there enclosed with railings and almost hidden from sight by trees. It is located quite a long way from the school and the then Royal Hospital, and it must have been very hard work for boys and pensioners to haul the heavy, loaded hand-carts carrying the water such a distance. When gas lighting was installed it took the place of candles which were the only means of illumination, and one can imagine that when the sanitary arrangements were connected to the sewers it was a great improvement (see fig. 4).

Towards the latter end of the century fewer boys were being accepted into the Royal Navy; the very prime object of the school was not being fulfilled.

During the century officers began to get the opportunity to specialise. It started in H.M.S. *Excellent* in 1830, for gunnery, followed by engineers being awarded commissions in 1847, and as the Navy passed from sail to steam, and from ship-of-the-line to Dreadnought, various other specialists

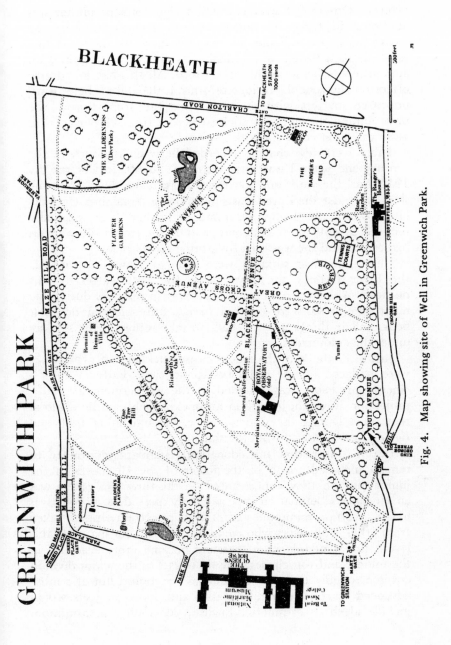

Fig. 4.   Map showing site of Well in Greenwich Park.

evolved. Others fell into extinction. The rank of master was abolished in 1864; his duties were then carried out by the navigating lieutenant and the master's mate by the navigating sub-lieutenant (even this branch was to fall into disuse, no appointments being made after 1883). All this had an adverse effect on the school. Various reforms at the end of the century improved matters with the result that the proportion of the boys joining the navy or dockyards rose from 28 per cent. in 1885 to 76 per cent. in 1906.

There were few changes recorded between the turn of the century and when I was there during 1926–30. Just before the 1914 War, the yards and top masts were taken down from the ship, with just the lower masts and rigging remaining. Over the latter years the living accommodation had been gradually reduced to only sleeping aboard, and by the end of the War this had ceased and she was used for storing sports gear.

During the War supplies were brought from Deptford via the River Thames, the boys taking the 32ft. cutter for this purpose. Whenever a Zeppelin raid was in progress during the night, the boys were ordered to lay fully clothed on their beds, and if things got too bad, to take refuge in the subway under the colonnades.

Just after the War, the quick-release buckled boots (plate 22) were replaced by the ordinary lace-up type. Early in 1926 a cinema projector was installed in the gymnasium, at 170ft. projection, it was the longest in Europe, probably in the world at that time. During the summer leave, the remaining masts and rigging were removed from the ship.

During this period the educational standards continued to remain high. Although in the lower of the 10 classes of the junior division they concentrated on the three 'Rs' (there was an entrance examination that had to be passed, so no one was below a certain minimum except perhaps certain orphans taken from other orphanages who could not at that time get up to this level), the standards soon rose and became more academic in the middle and top classes. The six classes of the senior division covered roughly the same syllabus as the junior, but at a more advanced level. The middle classes and above subjects would include algebra, arithmetic, English, geography, mensuration,

1. A Greenwich boy, 1791-94.

MARCHING TO THE DINING HALL.

2. Lower School marching to the Dining Hall.

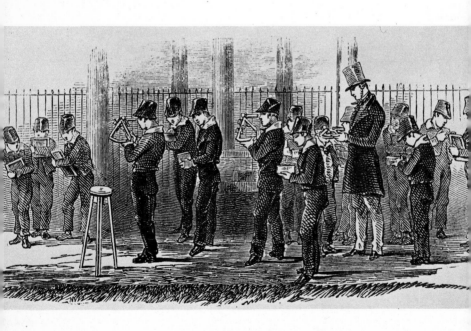

3. The Nautical Division, 1848.

4. The Old School Chapel.

5. The College Chapel.

6. The School Observatory.

7. Taking observations at the Observatory.

8. The Dining Hall.

9. The Dining Hall—3rd cooks with Tea Kettles.

10. A classroom about 1890.

11. A Dormitory about 1890.

12. Wash lavatories.

13. The Gymnasium.

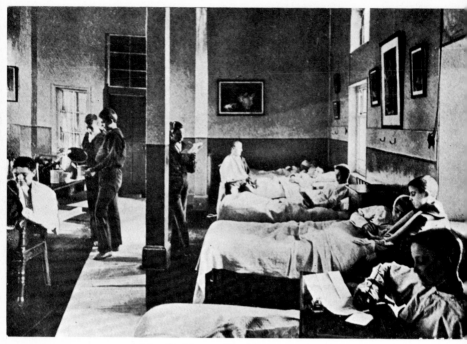

14. Up Home—Top Wards about 1890.

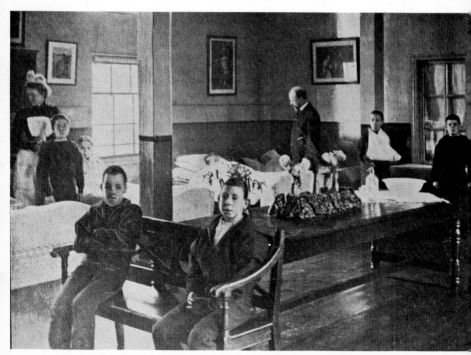

15. Up Home—Bottom Wards about 1890.

reading, scripture, trigonometry and geometry. Wherever practical, logarithm tables were used. The advanced class curriculum included navigation, and a copy of a summer term examination paper with possible marks is as follows:

	Marks
Algebra	100
Arithmetic	100
Drawing	100
English	100
Geography	100
Mensuration	50
Navigation	100
Physics	100
Poetry	50
Reading	100
Scripture	100
Dictation	100
Trigonometry	100
Writing	50
Geometry	100
Total	1,350

The Upper Nautical School, which included in its classes the Boreman Company, had a similar syllabus to the advance class, but included engineering drawing, astronomical observation, and surveying. Practical lessons of the latter subject were carried out in the school grounds and Greenwich Park.

As the plans for the move to the new school at Holbrook began to materialise during this period, the Boreman Company began to be run down. The boys leaving were not replaced by local 'day boys' but by enlarging the Upper Nautical Company (No. 9 Company). There was a limit to the number that could be accommodated in No. 9 Company's dormitory, so arrangements were made for the boys who were successful in the entrance examination to retain their company number and keep to their original sleeping and domestic arrangements. They paraded, dined, and took part in all other activities with No. 9 Company.

In 1921 Mr. Gifford Sherman Reade presented his estate of nearly 900 acres at Holbrook, near Ipswich, to the Admiralty in gratitude for the fact that not one of his fleet of tea ships had been sunk in the 1914–18 War. When he died in 1929 he left his residuary estate as an endowment for the school. This magnificent new school with its spacious surroundings was completed in 1931, and the transfer of the boys from the old to the new took place on 22 March 1933 (see plate 43).

The last boy to be a pupil of Greenwich Royal Hospital School to leave the new school at Holbrook was Jack Jermyn Dunn. He joined the school at Greenwich in October 1932 and quickly passed into the Upper Nautical Division. He moved with the school to Holbrook, and left to an appointment in H.M. Dockyard, Portsmouth, on 5 November 1937. He is shown wearing his Upper Nautical uniform in the photograph (see plate 41).

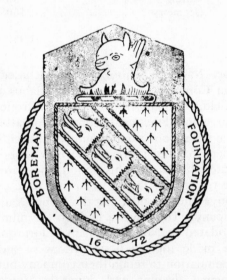

Chapter Three

THE BOREMAN COMPANY

IN 1672 SIR WILLIAM BOREMAN founded the Greencoat Collegiate School for 20 boys on the north side of London Street (now Greenwich High Road), near the junction of South Street, and skirting Prince of Orange Lane. For approximately two hundred years it continued to educate both collegers and fee-paying day boys (see fig. 1, p. 3).

As the school was to have a naval education bias, there is evidence that Sir William persuaded his friend Samuel Pepys, the famous Secretary to the Navy, to accompany him to Greenwich to fix the curriculum. He did this on the same lines as the school founded by the Duke of York and himself a short time before, which is reputed to have been the first school of its type.

In addition to being Secretary of the Navy, Samuel Pepys was a governor of Christ's Hospital, and from him Sir William decided the school uniform to be buckled shoes, yellow stockings, knee-breeches, jacket, coat, belt, and hat. The hat and long coat were to be of a similar shade to that of the green cloth which covers the table around which sit the Board of the Green Cloth. The foundation was governed by the Drapers' Company. The green coats were decorated with a badge showing Sir William's personal coat-of-arms, which consisted of a shield, within which was a golden diagonal parallel enclosing three boars' heads, and surrounded with ermine (opposite).

He (Pepys) would also have recommended the school attendance times: 7 a.m. to 11 a.m., and 1 p.m. to 5 p.m., preceded and closed by prayers. There were exercises in the evening, and attendance at Greenwich church for a service on Saturday afternoons, and morning and evening service on Sundays.

An eye-witness account of a Sunday service in 1719 shows 'that St. Alphage Church was crowded with worshippers' and

'In the South Gallery the girls sat "behind in ye room" and
the Green and Grey Coat Boys [Roan School] "behind in ye
West End" '. 'In pew 12 sat Mrs. Hudson and her scholars. In
pew 11 North sat Mr. Preddy and his School' and 'In pew 12
next ye middle, Mrs. Norman and her scholars'.

To qualify for admission to the school one had to be born in
Greenwich, and to be the son of a seaman, waterman or fisher-
man. The school fees for day boys at the time were around 10s.
a quarter or £2 a year. It was the first recorded school at
Greenwich, and the first navigation school in England, possibly
in the world. Christ's Hospital (Bluecoats) established a navigation class in that school in 1673 and was a close second.

In 1860 it is recorded 'That the Church of St. Alphage was
pictured filled with men and women handsomely dressed. On
one side of the organ sat the Greycoat boys and girls, on the
other side sat the Greencoat boys and the Bluecoat girls. The
latter wearing white short-shoulder-capes and long white
mittens, grey stockings and black shoes. The schoolmaster had
"to bring his scholars to Church every Sunday at the beginning
of prayers before 'the bell had done ringing' "' and present
names of those who do not attend. The boys in their long grey
coats and well-polished shoes, marching along Turnpin Lane to
the church, whilst the Green Coat boys and the Blue Coat girls
came to the church from the opposite direction'.

The boys were accepted (as nominees of Sir William Boreman) into the Upper Nautical School of the Greenwich Royal
Hospital School in 1886, for which there was an annual sub-
scription of £10 per annum for every boy admitted. The school
uniform consisted of a peak cap with badge on the front (gold
lace with W.B. interwoven, laurel leaves left and right and a
crown on top), Eton jacket and brass buttons, trousers, and a
double-breasted pea jacket, all navy blue.

An 'Old Boreman' boy records, 'I sat for the Boreman
Foundation Scholarship in 1912 and entered the Upper
Nautical School the same year. The competitive education
examination took place in a room at the Northern end of the
West Wing. Those who were sucessful on the first day were told
to report for a medical examination on next day; eyes, nose,
throat, heart, lungs, height, straight legs, arms and back.

Hammer toes, knock-knees, pigeon-chests etc. were items of failure. About thirty sat for the exam but only nine eventually were successful.

'There was homework every evening and it was a rare occasion when we only had to take home two books, mostly it was four and two of them would certainly be Geometry and French. We carried the books home strapped together with straps supplied for the purpose; schoolbags were never used.

'Behaviour outside the school gates was as strict as inside the school gates. We were never allowed to walk more than two abreast along the pavements, neither were we allowed to "hop the wag" or "thumb a lift". Neither were we allowed out improperly dressed, hat on the back of the head, jacket buttons undone, or carrying jackets etc. No shouting, wrestling, or horseplay of any kind was allowed in the streets, the Petty Officers saw to that. They could award half-hour-stands, which meant standing on the stage in the Gymnasium for thirty minutes, or they could be reported to the Headmaster for his disciplinary action'.

By 1926, the uniform worn was the same as the rest of the Upper Nautical School. The round 'sailor's' cap had succeeded the peaked cap. The cap ribbon bore the legend 'The Boreman Foundation', the bow of which was worn over the left ear.

The last Boreman day boy to leave Greenwich Royal Hospital School was George Frederick Berry (B.56), who entered in May 1927 and left to join H.M.S. *Fisgard* as E.R.A. apprentice in December 1931 (see plate 40).

Chapter Four

THE SHIP

THE FIRST THING one noticed when one entered the school grounds, and perhaps the most striking 'building', was the 'Ship'. It had been reduced to being used as a store, long before my time, but it had been a home and training establishment for thousands of boys in the past. I have gathered together the scanty information and photographs that seem to be available, and will devote the next few pages to the *Fame* (see plates 16-21).

The first ship, a *Sloop of War,* was built at Chatham on wooden sleepers and, after construction, dismantled and, in 1843, rebuilt in the school grounds. She had 10 ports on each side, with bridle ports and eight long guns. The figurehead was from Anson's ship *Centurion,* which was a great pity, for this valuable relic was allowed to deteriorate, and was destroyed in a very short time. In the copy of the engraving (see plate 16) she is seen going into action under her three top-sails, with hands aloft loosening the top-gallant sails. One can imagine the boys below, hauling on the tackles to run the guns out, others standing by with long-handled mops, rammers, etc., all preparing to 'open fire' on the imaginary enemy. Cutlasses and pikes would be served out to the boarding parties, for I read 'that cutlasses and staves were used during drill practice'. This vessel lasted fewer than sixteen years, for in 1859 'there was a walled-in area, oval in shape, extending from the Queen's House, to a point near the gates, which separated the Upper School, which was for the sons of Officers of the Royal Navy and Royal Marines, from the lower school which was for the sons of Ratings'. In 1862 the second ship was built. The only record I can find is in 1863. 'We in the third year at the School have gun drill aboard the *Fame* and went aloft furling sails . . .'. This ship lasted fewer than ten years. I imagine the reason for the short lives of these two ships was

26

the inadequate protection against rot from rising damp (see plate 17).

In 1872 the third and last vessel was built. This work was carried out by Messrs. Silley, Green and Wear, of Surrey Docks, now known as R. & H. Green and Silley Wear Ltd., whose records unfortunately were destroyed by enemy action during the Second World War, so all the details are lost.

She was a corvette of 400 tons, three masted, and fully rigged (square rigged on all three masts); the figure-head was *Fame* holding her long trumpet. There were two crews on this vessel, 100 from the Upper School and 100 from the Nautical School (see plate 20).

Crewed as a normal man-of-war of the period, watches were kept, and time was indicated by ringing the bell at half-hourly intervals. Entering and leaving harbour routine, including heaving the lead, was practised and when in harbour it was 'hands over the side to paint ship'. Action Stations still included gun drill, and making and setting sails; in fact life was as near as possible the same as if the crew were on active service at sea. The only departure from reality was that nets were hung all around the sides to catch any unfortunate who might fall from aloft. The photographs (plates 20 and 21) show the ship under sail, with a good example of sail repairs, probably carried out by the boys, and of manning the yards.

Just before 1914-18 War, the yards were taken down, the crews were reduced to boys in their last six months of training, and meals were taken in the Upper Nautical Dining Room with the Number Nine Company. Climbing up the rigging to the masthead each morning was still continued and life was lived as near as possible to naval routine. There was no gun drill at this time, but the boys slept in hammocks, carried out boatwork, and lived all the ship life that could be reproduced in the circumstances.

Over the next 10 years the masts and rigging were gradually reduced, until in August 1926 the three remaining stumps and rigging were removed. No one was allowed aboard during my stay at the school, not even to retrieve a ball that might have accidentally been kicked onto the deck. If we compare the age of this last ship with its predecessors she must have been in an advanced state of decay by this time, although she seemed sound enough from the outside.

An Old Boy recalls the day he saw the ship being demolished: '. . . I watched the wrecking of the 'Fame' by cross-cut saw and sledge hammer. For over fifty years the ship had been looked upon as one of the sacred institutions representative of our great Country and for what it stood. It seemed part of our very soul and, under many foreign skies, a thousand returning thoughts of the dear old ship have touched the heart-strings and comforted many lonely wanderers and exiles'.

Some of the best timbers were selected for cutting into small two-inch cubes, on which were fixed metal plates suitably inscribed with the history of the ship; they sold for half-a-crown each. The figurehead and bowsprit were taken to the new school at Holbrook, Suffolk, and incorporated in the rifle range building.

An American millionaire and his wife were at the time visiting England with a view to purchasing some historic naval items for a Maritime Museum at Newport News, U.S.A., which he was in the course of building. During their stay in London somebody casually told them that if they cared to go down to Greenwich they might find something of interest as a lot of old naval junk was being broken up, burnt, or thrown on the rubbish dump.

During the course of his visit to Greenwich, where he stayed for a few weeks, he purchased the circular plaque, which formed the stern decoration of the *Fame*, the anchor, bell, and various other items including some of the structure between decks. In due course the items were transported to what is known as the 'Treasure of Virginia'. This museum at Newport News is overlooking the James River, which the first colonists from England to the New World named for their king, James I. Newport News obtained its name from Captain Christopher Newport and his three little ships which sailed from Greenwich, the *Godspeed,* the *Discovery,* and the *Susan Constant*.

PART TWO

Chapter One

THE ARRIVAL

THE TRAIN DREW TO A HALT at London Bridge Station. Steam mingled with the hazy October sunshine that streamed down through the glass roof. Alighting, my aunt and I made our way to the waiting room, which in those days boasted a cheerful coal fire, to wait for the train which was to take us on the final leg of our journey to Greenwich. I carried a cheap cardboard attache case containing a packet of writing paper and envelopes costing one penny, one three-halfpenny stamp and a toothbrush.

My mind travelled back over the events that had led to this journey, which would divorce me from my friends, home, family, my entire past, and would bring me into a completely new life and environment.

Until five years previously ours had been a normal family. My father was usually at sea on the Australia run, on ships that later were to be written into history—*Jarvis Bay, Empress Bay,* etc., on trips that took about fourteen weeks. My mother, younger brother, then two years old, and my sister, aged about three months, all shared a house with my maternal grandparents in Southsea. Up to this time the arrival of my father, loaded with presents, was a great occasion, especially once when he arrived with a parrot. Every month my mother would draw her money through the local bank—we were indeed fortunate in those dark days of unemployment just after the First World War.

It was my birthday, 24 August 1923. My father had given me a watch, and an atlas to plot his voyages; he kissed me 'goodbye' as he had to leave the following morning—we never saw him again. Some weeks later, my mother was informed that my father had 'disappeared' from the ship and her payments had now ceased. In a short time we were destitute, her savings gone. She looked desperately for work—washing, scrubbing floors, needlework, anything.

During the war she had made sailors' collars, working for the Admiralty, and although the work had been exacting, there had been no need to rush things and she had been able to take her time. She now applied again and was fortunate to be given a quota to make. The standard of work now required was unbelievably difficult; there were now many measurements that had to be strictly correct, by far the worse being the three tapes which were to be sewn on at eight stitches to the inch, and no tolerance allowed. A fraction out (the tape was marked with blue crayon) and not only had the work to be re-done but the cost of the tape was deducted from her pay. It took three hours to complete one collar for which she was paid ninepence. Only able to work by daylight (no electric light in most houses in those days), she worked from dawn to dusk, never leaving her seat by the window even for meals. During the first few weeks there were many rejects, and there were many tears shed.

It was at about this time that she applied to the Board of Guardians (the parish) for help. This was usually given in the form of a meal voucher valued at five shillings. We made our appearance, and after listening to our tale of woe were told, 'You and your children's place is in the "House" [workhouse]'. Stunned, my mother never asked for charity again from anyone, the exception being the Brotherhood Boot Fund which supplied us with boots once a year. The luxuries of the mayor's Christmas parcels and various other charities were not for us.

During those lean years some of the shopkeepers were very good to us, in spite of their own difficulties. I remember my grandmother saying very often after I had brought back a copper's-worth of 'mixed vegetables', 'Mr. C. has served the boy well, Mary, almost enough for two meals'; and after bones had been bought for a nominal sum, 'There's a fair piece of meat on this one, Mary, almost a joint'. A kindly fishmonger, noticing my brother with his large heavy boots hanging on spindly legs, a pale thin face under a large cap called, 'Can you do with a kipper, Alf?' Alf, of course, was not my brother's name; but we had kipper for tea. Thereafter a fish of some kind was often given with a similar enquiry as to 'Alf's' taste. It became quite a byword in our house, the kindness behind all this not being realised by myself until many years later.

In spite of our financial difficulties, our upbringing was not neglected. We always had our Sunday-best clothes, which if not new, were only worn on special occasions. Both my grandparents held strong religious and moral beliefs, and we were brought up to be Godfearing and fair-dealing. We went to Sunday school twice on Sundays, and as we neared Christmas I usually managed to share my attendances with another establishment ensuring that an extra tea party was going to be one of the bounties given to the good. I chose, however, the wrong one on one occasion as, apart from being a poor do, the present off the tree turned out to be a pair of braces and gentleman's size at that.

My regular church was St. Michael's, now sadly demolished, and I decided to join the choir which, apart from playing an important part in this story, enabled me to bring home my first wage of twopence per month. It was some time during the following year, whether it was the minister who had suggested it to me, or vice versa, I cannot remember, that I had the idea that if I went to a training school the financial burden at home would be eased. One day I asked him if he would be kind enough to visit my mother to discuss my future, and when he called it was with a deep sense of dread of leaving home, and a great outward show of unconcern, that I listened to the various establishments, their possiblities and merits. It was finally decided that Greenwich Royal Hospital School should be approached, and after the preliminary educational and medical examinations had been passed I was provisionally accepted, and was now on my way.

Our train finally arrived, and we started the last part of the journey, the unfamiliar congested scenery of factories, church spires and humble backyards passed by until we arrived at Greenwich station. A short rolling ride in the local tram took us to the gates of my new home. As we alighted, the school grounds seemed to stretch as far as the eye could see either way; fronted by rather tall cast-iron railings behind which a thick privet-type hedge almost hid the wide parade ground with the

large stone buildings in the background. As we approached the
large openwork double gateway, the first thing I noticed was
the ship. This was built into the concrete, its bowsprit pointing
like a huge finger towards us. Just inside the gate, on the left-
hand side, was a sentry box in which were two boys dressed in
the naval rig of the school. Just outside had gathered a cluster
of boys with their parents talking to the officer in charge of
the gate. He was rather tall, very red faced, a man of about
fifty years, dressed in the uniform of a naval petty officer (as
all company officers were dressed), and as we found out later
was known as 'Tug' Wilson. The required number to make up a
batch having now arrived, we were marched off in a somewhat
disorderly fashion across the parade ground, through a kind of
shrubbery-come garden to the extreme western boundary where
we entered a two-storeyed building which was the hospital, the
ground floor of which housed the surgery.

We entered a very long, narrow room (called the Long Room).
The walls were painted the usual buff colour used in schools at
the time, and on one wall were fixed several wash-basins and a
kind of large trough for washing feet. The other side was bare
with the exception of a door and a window; on the sill of the
latter stood five large glass jars of medicine, more of which we
shall hear later. Below this window was a cloth-covered table with
enamel containers of instruments, a glass container of bandages,
the jars of ointment, and on a shelf near the window brewed a
highly-polished copper steriliser. At the far end of the room,
behind a small partition, was a space where the doctor made
his examinations. There was a desk, balance-type scales, eye-
testing charts, and it was at this end of the room that we
gathered. We stripped off all our clothes except our trousers
and there were two medical attendants who hovered around
keeping us in order until the surgeon arrived. He was a slight,
white-haired, cultured-looking man. He looked the ideal
doctor or priest, and as he took his seat at the desk, I noticed
his four gold bands with red between which told me that
he was a surgeon captain (see plate 25). In due course my
turn came for examination; it was only a superficial affair
as we had all passed a medical previously. I finally mounted
the scales.

'Hm, hm', from the surgeon. 'Not much meat on your bones, m'lad'. 'No, sir', I replied.

'You don't seem very strong to me, not fit enough for our requirements; what would you say if I failed you?'

'You cannot do that, sir', I protested, and as briefly as possible told him of the desperate circumstances we were in. A gentle hand was placed on my shoulder. 'Now, I will pass you on one condition, you must get more meat on those bones. Eat all you can.'

He seemed a very kind man. Having satisfied himself that we were all fit and that we were not introducing any ailments into the establishment, we all donned our clothes and we were led off to the stores to be kitted up.

A peculiar smell of serge and other naval items struck the nose as I entered the gloomy room. Passing along a counter, I received in turn blue serge suit and knitted jumper; 'move along'; flannel vest and long pants; 'move along'; socks and boots placed on top of the pile, and so on until the issue was complete. I changed into my new clothes, the rough naval flannel underwear against my skin, the unyielding heavy army-type boots on my feet. My heart sank still lower—I would never get used to this. Wearing our No. 2 blue suits, and with our discarded civvies in a bag, we marched towards the gate and to our friends, who now, of course, could not distinguish one from another until we were quite close to them. By the look on my aunt's face, she wasn't very happy with the change. We marched out of the gate and proceeded some quarter of a mile to what was to be our home for the next three weeks: Trafalgar Quarters. I bade my aunt a fond farewell, and she took my few civvy clothes. My new life had started.

Chapter Two

TRAFALGAR QUARTERS (See plate 35)

NOW MAY BE the opportunity to fit my aunt into the story. She was two years younger than my mother, and her complete opposite. She had fair hair, blue eyes and a roundish face, and was not one that could be called the domestic type. She preferred to move around rather than reside in one place. Married, she had a daughter a little older than my sister, who lived most of her younger life with my family. Her husband, a fine craftsman and a specialist in his particular profession, worked in London, being unable to find his particular type of work locally, and moved around to wherever he could find accommodation near his work. Although they owned a house in Southsea, it was let, and when she could not get rooms with her husband, she came down to stay with us. This arrangement helped my grandparents financially, and without this aid I do not know how they would have managed. I was her favourite and she often slipped the odd penny into my hand. It was aunt, therefore, who, knowing her way around London, was chosen to accompany me on this occasion.

There are many pictures of Greenwich College with its imposing twin domes, usually viewed from the Thames. It is situated on the south side of the Thames, between the bank of the river and Greenwich Park. The school was on the edge of the park and separated from the college by Romney Road, where I had so recently arrived by tram.

Trafalgar Quarters is situated in Park Row which runs along the eastern boundary of the complex from the park to the river. It is reputed to be on the site, opposite the eastern gate of the college, where Sir Walter Raleigh spread his cloak in the mud to protect Queen Elizabeth I from soiling her shoes. Two storeys high, it is built of dark bricks with stone copings. The top floor is set well back, with arched windows, and there is a fine stone crest carved in the enlarged centre parapet.

A kind of cloister surrounds the ground floor, formed by brick arches on the sides, and on the front elevation these are supplemented by pairs of stone pillars which form a central feature matching the crest on the stone pediment.

As soon as things had quietened down, we were summoned into the common room. This was a large room, completely bare of furniture apart from a single row of lockers which ran along each long wall from end to end. They were numbered, odd numbers on the right, evens on the left. We were formed into two lines by our new company officer and told to stand one to a locker, into which we placed our surplus kit. We were now told that 'Those who are on the right and have odd numbers are Starboard, and those even and on the left are Port, and that will ever be so. So remember—Starboard Watch prepare tea'.

The dining room was reached through the door at the far end of the common room. It was furnished with several long 'mess' tables and stools which, together with the floor, had been scrubbed to a brilliant white finish. At the wall end of each table stood a pile of pewter plates and several rows of white china basins (dips). On the centre of each table stood a salt and pepper pot and water jug, which were of pewter, and at the other end a large kettle, or dixie, as it is known in the army. I picked up a kettle and went to the kitchen to collect the tea for my mess while the loaves, which were somewhat smaller than civvy small-size ones, were being cut into thirds and a dab of margarine placed on each. These were then placed around the table, each with a knife and plate. When the dips had been half filled with what could be called tea, the lads were called in, and those who felt like eating commenced their first meal. After the tables had been cleared, we spent the rest of the evening either in the common room or the small ground outside. I wandered around looking at the unfamiliar faces, boys of between 10 and 12 years of age, all dressed alike; one now rather noticed the colour of the hair.

'Where do you come from?' enquired a youngster about the same age as myself.

'Portsmouth', I replied. 'And you?'

'Bristol.'

'What's your name?' he asked.

'Dan Turner—and yours?'

'Jack Townsend', and, after a moment, 'would you like to see some of my comics?'

'Yes, please.'

He reminded me very much of a fellow classmate I once knew in Portsmouth. He went over to his locker and he rummaged around his few belongings. I noticed that he was somewhat shorter than myself, and a rather thick set lad with extremely fair hair and light blue eyes. I asked him why he had decided to join. His answer implied that, unlike myself, he had been eager to embark upon this type of career and was looking forward to the time when he could swagger around Bristol, and, in due course, join the Navy. Anyway that was his story (which I fully believed), and I would have probably said something similar if asked. Thus began a friendship that was to last, with one or two breaks, the whole time I was at the school. I later found out that his mother had died some time before, and that his father had recently remarried. I did not at the time appreciate his loss, as my father had been at sea almost continually for the first four years of my life, during the war (and I had not seen him at all until I was three years old). He had been away most of the time since, so I did not miss him as I would have done had it been my mother.

It was soon bedtime, and after we had assembled we marched into the dormitory. There were several rows of beds with a small white number painted on each; my number being '1' was nearest to the door. I made up my bed and with the others said prayers; and with the C.O.'s voice ringing 'Silence is to be maintained in the dormitory at all times', he lowered the lights and left us to our thoughts. The unfamiliar surroundings—the smell of Navy soap which impregnated the bed linen, the soft mumbling of someone whispering to his neighbour—kept me awake for a long time. It had been a long and eventful day. My mind wandered to my home and family, and the long journey. It was then that I realised that I had left my case at the station when we changed at London Bridge. I had no money and no means of writing home. I really felt cut off and abandoned. With those thoughts I eventually fell asleep.

'Rise and shine', bawled the C.O., almost in my ear, for he was standing in the doorway. 'Come on, jump to it, the sun is scorching your eyes out'.

It seemed to be the middle of the night, but it was, in fact, six o'clock, far earlier than I had ever risen before. I hastily donned shirt, trousers and socks, and with my boots in my hand dashed out with the rest to the wash lav. A wash in tepid water, return to re-make my bed, breakfast, and I was ready for what fate had in store for me this day. The first day.

The morning was spent having our hair cut, convict style, and being taught the rudiments of parade drill. The afternoon, more drill and a short march along some of the nearby roads. On the second day, after our usual half hour of forming fours, etc., we were marched over to the main school where we made our way to the surgery and the long room. We were all stripped to the waist (and this was where I realised the disadvantage of being No. 1) and waited for the next move. It was to be vaccination. I received my jab, given by the doctor, after which the attendant beckoned me over to the window which housed the medicine bottles.

'White Mixture or Black Jack?' he asked. Although the colours were obviously opposite, the results were intended to be the same.

'Black Jack', I replied. It somehow had a better-sounding, nautical name. I downed the unpleasant liquorice-tasting concoction, the dozens of pairs of eyes following every grimace I made.

'Get dressed and wait outside', I was told, and from a vantage point outside the window I could now watch the two attendants issuing the medicine.

One was a thick-set middle-aged man, his black hair plastered straight back from his forehead. He wore thick horn-rimmed spectacles, rather unusual in those days. Later I was to find out his name was Mr. Pike. He was rather a quiet man who worked deftly, and it seemed untiringly, with his many patients. His counterpart was a rather older man, his craggy features instilling a certain amount of fear in one which a defect in one eye did not tend to dispel. When roused, or when things became rather boisterous in the long room, he would really bristle, and woe betide the unfortunate he was attending to. He was rather tall, and moved with rather sharp, jerky, impatient movements, and he certainly stood no nonsense. I was to find that he wielded tweezers, lance and scissors on boils and other small abscesses with some flamboyance. He was known throughout the school as Crimmy (Criminal) (see plate 25). He always treated me with consideration, except that he had a grudge against a small mole close to the left side of my nose. Its removal offered a challenge to Crimmy, and during the next three years, at intervals, he tried everything. First time, a straight tug off with the tweezers followed by a dash of iodine; on other occasions, a snip with the scissors followed by dabs of various salves, ointments, or whatever he thought of at the moment. Finally, attempts at cauterising with various acids. It defied all his attempts, and when shaving I can still see one of Crimmy's failures.

We were marched back to our quarters, and after our midday meal dressed in our number ones. These were our best suits, which were blue serge jumpers and bell-bottom trousers. In summer the only underclothes worn was a flannel shirt with the front, trimmed with blue braid round the neckline, showing. In winter we wore in addition flannel underpants, and over the flannel shirt a knitted blue jersey which fitted closely round the neck and presented a dark navy-blue front, which was surrounded by the front of the sailor's collar with its three white tapes. A black silk, folded to about an inch and a half width, went round the neck under the collar, down the front, and was tied at the bottom of the vee with two tapes called 'fancies'. Caps were only worn with number ones, black in the winter, white in summer. White cap covers (pudding bags) were issued, but to wear one was considered the very lowest form. This rig was worn only on Sundays, on special occasions, and when one went outside the school. Number twos were, after the first issue, the old number ones, worn at classes, parades and all other occasions except work and play. The blue jumpers had collars of the same material tailored to them and, of course, were covered by the 'real' collars when our best rig was worn.

The third suit was made of canvas and called 'ducks', being the same style as the blues, but not tailored to fit, and was, of course, white. With twos which were worn at classes, or duck suits, which were for work and play, blue and white striped shirts were worn to keep jersey or flannel clean. In winter long navy flannel underpants were worn.

At last we were fully dressed, in two ranks and ready to march out. Not an inspiring sight, nor cause for alarm to Britain's enemies, for we had not yet been to the tailors to have our suits finally fitted; therefore baggy trousers and roomy jumpers were the rig of the day. We marched along the river-front, where the sight of the water and the ships was very comforting to me as it somehow acted as a link between home and myself. 'Are any of those ships going to Portsmouth?' I wondered.

The days passed: we soon settled-in to the routine—meals, drills, a few educational tests, visits to the hospital for various reasons, including an unpleasant trip to the dentist, but by far the best was our afternoon's march out.

I had been away from home now for just over a week and to my great delight I received a letter from home. 'Why had I not written, was I all right?' They were quite concerned at my silence and to see for themselves the actual state of affairs. Both my mother and grandfather were coming up on Sunday and would be arriving at about 1.30 p.m. I was delighted.

At last Sunday arrived and I waited impatiently as near the gate as I dare. The time arrived—2 p.m., 2.30, 3.00—as the afternoon passed my spirits dropped lower and lower until at about 3.30 p.m. I gave up hope and, leaning against the wall, head on arm, I gave way to a torrent of tears. All the pent-up emotions of the past days came to the surface, and my shoulders shook with anguish. It was in this unsailor-like state that they first saw me in uniform. They had, of course, lost themselves and travelled halfway around London before finding the school. Tears soon turned to smiles, and it was a great joy to see them. I didn't have the sense to tell the C.O. of my parent's visit, therefore it was only possible for them to stay for a very short time, because it was nearing our call to tea at 4 p.m., and to disobey an order, even at this early stage, was unthinkable.

Two major things happened at that visit; they brought me a 'ditty box' (which I still have) and it was agreed that whatever happened, I would write home on Sundays and Wednesdays, and would receive a letter on Tuesdays and Fridays. We never failed to keep to this arrangement throughout the next four years, although there were occasions when mother received hers without a stamp. (I would enclose a silver three-penny piece if I had the money but could not get a stamp in time.)

The day that had the most lasting effect on me was when we visited the College. During the brief visits to the main school I had noticed the grandeur of the buildings designed by Wren on the opposite side of Romney Road, especially the impressive twin towers, and now we were going to be able to have a look at close quarters at not only the outside but also inside the beautiful Painted Hall and chapel.

There were no buildings of such excellence in my home town and the splendour of their interiors and paintings opened my eyes to the world of art and good taste. I was excited to be near Nelson's relics, especially the clothes that he died in, and I was proud to be even remotely associated with such surroundings. We passed over to the chapel, viewed the famous spiral staircase which winds its way up the clock tower, past the marble pillars and into the chapel itself, of which I shall say more later.

Our last visit was to the Observatory (which was long before the establishment was moved to Sussex). As we climbed the hill the huge domes, which housed the giant telescopes and are one of the main features of the building, became more detailed. At the base of a short mast at the top of the tower is a black ball which, a few seconds before midday, ascends to the top, and after a brief wait descends, pauses halfway for a second, signifying noon precisely, then drops to the base. There were many other items of interest and the panoramic view of London: the school below us, the College across the road, backed by the river, the Isle of Dogs, and in the far distance the jumble of chimneys and buildings merging into a smoky mist. It was as well we had a good look around, for it was to be the last occasion for some time on which we would be free to do so because the time had now come to move to the main school.

When we had first arrived at Trafalgar Quarters we had each been allocated to a particular company, and given our own number in it. My company was No. 7, and in it I was No. 84, 7/84. Each company was named after a famous admiral; we were 'H' for Howe, and all my clothes were therefore marked H.7/84 as a laundry mark. It was after our midday meal on Wednesday when, with all our belongings, we assembled together for the last time as one unit, and marched the short distance (somewhat smarter than when we had first travelled the opposite way) to our new home.

Chapter Three

THE SCHOOL*†

WE CAME TO A HALT outside what we were to know as
'The Office', and after a few brief instructions, were dismissed
to our own devices. As it was 'make and mend' or half-day off
the whole complement of the school, some nine hundred boys,
was now to be seen for the first time. There were some improvised football matches (the proper ones being played in the
park), and other games being played. Some boys were on
roller-skates, weaving about between the players, some just
chasing one another around, while others were walking or
talking in groups. The scene and noise was rather overwhelming
after our three weeks of isolation.

A few boys had gathered to see the 'new jacks' arrive. There
were solicitous enquiries to which company one belonged,
and would we like to be shown around, always with the
weather-eye on the bundles we carried which might contain
some 'tuck'. Three or four of us of No. 7 company were soon
heading for the gymnasium where the canteen was situated.
Passing the two huge green painted doors, we entered. Buff-
coloured, latticed, curved girders spanning the spacious roof
reminded one of the inside of an airship, as one's gaze travelled
along the roof lights to the far end, where the motto 'Fear God
and Honour the King', together with the school crest, all in
red and gold, formed the top of the proscenium arch of a
stage. The stage itself, nearly filling the whole width of the
gymnasium was separated from the side walls by a narrow
passage and stairs. It was about four feet from ground level,
and the front, with the exception of a small door in the centre,
was made up of a four-row tier of lockers. These also extended
along both sides of the building, except for the exit doorways

*See plate 29
†See fig. 5

42

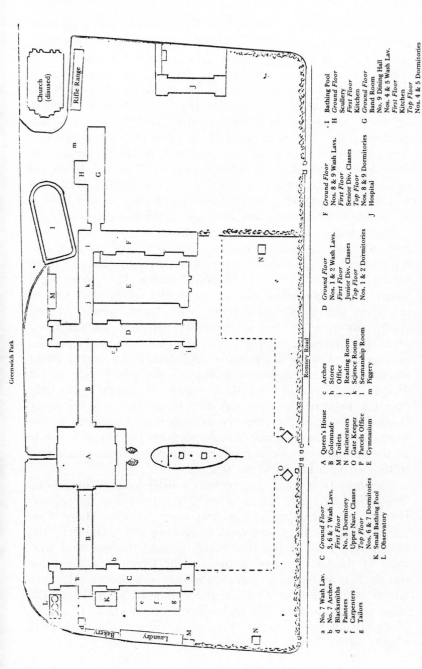

Fig. 5. Plan of school buildings.

a No. 7 Wash Lav.
b No. 7 Arches
d Blacksmiths
e Painters
f Carpenters
g Tailors

A Queen's House
B Colonnade
M Toilets
N Incinerators
O Gate Keeper
P Parcels Office
E Gymnasium

c Arches
h Stores
i Office
j Reading Room
k Science Room
l Seamanship Room
m Piggery

C *Ground Floor*
3, 6 & 7 Wash Lavs.
First Floor
No. 3 Dormitory
Upper Naut. Classes
Top Floor
Nos. 6 & 7 Dormitories
K Small Bathing Pool
L Observatory

D *Ground Floor*
Nos. 1 & 2 Wash Lavs.
First Floor
Junior Div. Classes
Top Floor
Nos. 1 & 2 Dormitories

F *Ground Floor*
Nos. 8 & 9 Wash Lavs.
First Floor
Senior Div. Classes
Top Floor
Nos. 8 & 9 Dormitories
J Hospital

I Bathing Pool
H *Ground Floor*
Scullery
First Floor
Kitchen
G *Ground Floor*
Band Room
No. 9 Dining Hall
First Floor
Nos. 4 & 5 Wash Lav.
Kitchen
Top Floor
Nos. 4 & 5 Dormitories

at the halfway mark. Along the whole of the left-hand side, about two feet in front of the lockers, ran a row of wallbars, giving that side of the room the appearance of a long cage. Above our heads, at the entrance, was a steel box structure which housed the cinematograph. On the front of the box was a clock, on the face of which was the legend *Tempus Fugit*; to me the legend seemed to operate during half days, holidays and Sundays only. The small pigeon-hole serving hatch was surrounded by customers eager to change postal orders or stamps into something more edible. On our right, fastened to the wall was the notice board and, in the corner, the instructor's 'cabin'. My locker was close at hand, being nearly at the end of the row, and I put in my few belongings and started to explore my new surroundings.

There was an entirely new atmosphere to get used to. The boys of Trafalgar Quarters were more or less of my own age, but some of my new colleagues were almost men, many of them having the physique of fully-grown adults. The games were tough, there were many rough-and-tumbles taking place here in the gym, and there was a general air of rushing and chasing about. My newly-found companions had left me for more promising pickings, and I decided to go back on to the parade, making my way to the bows of the ship. From here I could see that the main asphalted section of the parade was almost divided into two by the ship, which lay north and south, pointing towards the gate and the college respectively. Away from the stern of the ship the ground sloped upwards to the southern boundary which was formed by the Queen's House in the centre with the colonnades stretching from either side to two wings or blocks of the school.

This may be a good time to have a brief look at the general layout of the school. The main building consisted of the Queen's House, four wings or blocks and a gymnasium. There were subsidiaries, the large and small swimming baths, laundry, rifle range, etc. Two of the four wings formed the east and west sides of the parade: one, known as the Upper Nautical classrooms (C); the other, Junior Division classrooms (D), into which joined the far ends of the colonnade. Parallel to (D) were the gymnasium (E) and a matching block to C and D, block (F) known as Senior Division classrooms. The only block to run east and west contained the dining hall (G), and kitchen (H), which joined the main block roughly in line with the colonnade (see fig 5).

The building of the Queen's House was commissioned by James I in 1617 for his queen, Anne of Denmark, but when she died in 1619 the work was stopped. In 1629 Charles I ordered Inigo Jones, who designed the building, to complete the palace for his queen, Henrietta Maria, and it was completed in 1635. It is from her that the Queen's House derives its name. It is a two-storey building of stone, with a basement at ground level in the front. As the ground rises towards the park, the basement is completely hidden from view, and at the rear of the building the ground reaches ground floor level. In the front, there is a terrace, surrounded by balusters, from which two curved stairways lead down to the parade. It is from this terrace that the admiral takes the salute at march past.

The four main blocks were all of the same design, and in the main, were used for the same purpose. They were two-storey stone buildings matching the Queen's House in design. The top floors in all cases were used as dormitories. The first floors, with some exceptions were classrooms, and the ground floors were mainly used as wash-lavatories. The exceptions were: on the first floor of block (C), next to the Upper Nautical classrooms and below No. 6 dormitory, was No. 3 dormitory. At the northern end of the ground floor of block (D) was the office (i), with the stores (h) next door extending to the 'arches' (c). Block (G), which was adjacent and at right-angles to the Senior Division block, comprised of No. 4 dormitory on the top floor with the dining hall below, and No. 5 dormitory (H) with the kitchen below. Beneath the dining hall (partly underground), were Nos. 4 and 5 wash lavatories, No. 9 dining hall, and the band room. The scullery was under the kitchen, and an extension of the latter, approached from the ground floor by a flight of stone stairs, was the bread room, where the bread and margarine was served to the 'cooks'.

As we are mostly concerned with Nos. 6 and 7 companies, I will go into (C) block in further detail. No. 7 dormitory was at the southern end, and from my bed I could see into the park. No. 6 company occupied the other half of this floor. A spiral staircase separated the two halves of the building. As I have already said, No. 3 company's dormitory was on the first floor, next to the Upper Nautical classrooms. On the ground floor No. 7's wash lavatory was at the northern end of the block (a), Nos. 3 and 6 occupying the rest of the floor. The bath for the three companies was attached to No. 7 lavatory.

The ground floor of both C and D wings terminated at the colonnade, from where a subway ran underground, under the colonnade and Queen's House, connecting the two wings. This junction of stairs, subway and exits was known as 'The Arches', No. 7 arches on one side of the parade, but just 'the arches' on the Junior Division side. The latter provided a 'play area', and a short cut from the gymnasium to the parade ground. On either side of the spiral staircase the company officer's accommodation with the arches below formed two small wings, one on each side of the building. Our company officer, with his wife, occupied the top maisonette, the 'front door' of which came out onto the stairs halfway between the first and second floors, the doors to the bedrooms being on a higher level than the dormitory door. When leaving the dormitory one had to go down half a flight of stairs to the living quarters, or to the bedrooms, up what amounts to a half flight, and round a short landing.

The afternoon passed, and about four o'clock the bugle sounded what I was to find out was 'cooks'; this sent many of the boys scurrying towards the dining hall. About ten minutes later the bugle sounded the 'fall in' when there was a general rush to the gymnasium. Each company (approximately 115 boys in each) formed into two ranks, and had its allotted place, mine forming up at the stage end, with our backs to the wall-bars. The boy chief petty officer then proceeded to get some order into things.

'Company . . . 'shun', 'stand at . . . ease', 'company, 'shun', 'eyes . . . right'. There was some shuffling as we got ourselves into line and he quickly walked along the front rank, scanning to see that all was in order. 'Eyes front'.

Everything being to his satisfaction he smartly approached the company officer, giving a smart salute: 'No. 7 all correct, sir'. 'Carry on'. 'Stand at ease, no talking'.

One or two companies, not quite up to the mark, were being put through evolutions. Hoarse, impatient sounds of 'Form fours', 'Form two-deep' were heard.

While all this was in progress a lieutenant-commander had appeared on the stage, and one by one the company officers reported to him that all was correct. 'Carry on', from the stage (see plate 24).

'Number 8 company, right turn, double . . . march'. No. 8 doubled towards and disappeared into the space at the right-hand side of the stage.

It was our turn next. ' Number 7 company, left turn, right wheel, double . . . march.'

Caught in a tidal wave of bodies, I was hurtled past the stage, up the steps between stage and wall, along a corridor flanked on one side by more lockers, jostled up nine or ten stairs, and after a tight crush at the doorway, was propelled into the dining hall. Down the central aisle we sped and as we slowed down and thinned out at the other end, I noticed that the tables on either side each had a brass strip onto which the mess number was engraved and fastened to the end. Number 95, 96 at my number, 98, I turned into the space between the long stools to take my place at the 'mess'.

The dining hall (see plate 8), was a long tall room, the ceiling of which was divided into many panels, each containing a painting of some nautical scene or naval battle. The walls were pierced by large windows, between each of which were painted figures of famous mariners. Below the window sill level ran a continuous row of mess shelves. The top shelf, faced with brass, held the rows of spoons, 17 to a mess, all highly polished, like silver on gold. The two lower shelves held the basins (dips) and plates. The knife drawer fitted under the lower shelf, was immediately above the table. There were two shallow waste tins, water jug and the salt and pepper pots on the table, and the large dixie, or kettle as we called it, was on the floor at the end of the table, now doing duty as slop pan.

There were 120 messes; the tables and stools of plain deal wood scrubbed a gleaming white. Usually there were 17 boys to a mess, the captain being at the aisle end, his senior hand sitting opposite, and by seniority, religiously defined, to the lowest (mess shelf) end. It was of the utmost importance to get as high up the table as possible, because when the portions were served by the captain and passed down the line, they were carefully compared by each boy, the larger being retained and the smaller passed on, until by the time those at the mess shelf got their portion it was indeed the smallest. It was not unknown for a little picking to take place on the way down, so it really was a minute measure at times.

There was a space halfway along the room called the 'square'; it did not extend the full width, as the row of tables on one side of the hall formed one side. On the opposite side was the doorway to the kitchen and the stairs down to the scullery; above this exit was the organ loft. The only furniture on the square was a chair and a small table beside which stood the bugler.

'G' (quiet) was sounded, and the noise diminished. A rather slim-built company officer deftly climbed on to one of the tables opposite the square and gave a quick look either way. There was silence. 'Sam' had arrived. He had a thin face with a long aquiline nose. He reminded me of an eagle, and as he turned his head he leaned it to one side in rather a bird-like manner and, like the bird of prey, his eyes did not miss a thing. When he was suitably satisfied that it was perfectly quiet he gave a nod and grace was sung. It took me some days to find out what the words were—they sounded like 'Fall y be mercies' and with great gusto, 'May God's Holy Name be prais . . . ed'. Later, I noticed that it was displayed over the organ loft as 'For these and all His mercies, may God's Holy Name be praised'. At the midday meal, grace would be accompanied by the organ, and very pleasing it sounded. There were, however, occasions when for some unknown reason a section of the school would sing a few tones out of tune. What sparked it off each time I never did find out, but it was spontaneous in several parts of the hall at once. The resultant noise was hideous. Sam would wave his arms, everyone would stop singing, and on his signal recommence. Again the same row— more waving—silence. Sam would go very red in the face. Sometimes three or four attempts were made before the desired melody was achieved. It wasn't wise to misbehave during meal-times on these occasions. A nod from Sam, the bugler sounded the 'carry on', and we would scramble on to our stools and devour the fare as only hungry boys can.

There were two other new boys in my mess; this meant some argument to decide who was to be the fortunate one to gain one place up the table. Whether it was decided on age or alphabetical order I cannot now remember, but the result was that I had to sit at the mess shelf, and the third boy sat next to me. He was a quiet sort of a boy, rather on the tubby side; his number was 7/93. He relished the idea of his seniority and took every opportunity to show it.

During the meal Sam paced up and down the aisle, eyes missing nothing. The slightest sign of a comic or book (deady) being read, or any other misdemeanour, and a voice would roar, 'On the square . . . you'. The unfortunate would then have to double to the square to await punishment. This took the form of three heavy blows with a brush some eighteen inches long, the business end being about six inches by three, applied on the bottom while the recipient bent over a stool. This punishment brought tears to the eyes, and a straightened posture to the body.

'G' sounded. There was a scramble as we stood up by our places. A nod from Sam. 'Thanks be Un', which translated is 'Thanks be unto Thee O Lord' was sung. 'Advance' sounded, and we doubled out, not quite as madly as we entered, leaving the cooks to clear up, and the unfortunates on the square to their fate.

'Fall in' is soon sounded. We assemble in the gymnasium as before. This time we are marched out onto the parade ground, passing the bows of the ship, to our wash lavatory on the far side. Forming single file we enter. There are two double rows of basins set in beds of slate, and from the green painted racks over each hang the towels and tooth brushes. Each place is numbered. We strip to the waist (fortunately my place is near a window and I can put my clothes on the wide sill) and perform our ablutions each at the appropriate word of command. When we are finished and dismissed we make our way back to the gymnasium which we find is now locked.

As it is Wednesday, chairs are being set out, for it is picture night. Eventually the doors open and we pour in to get seated on chairs, lockers, wallbars, or the girders of the roof (my favourite place)—anywhere where one can get a good view. We settle down to an evening's entertainment. There is no music, but from time to time there are shouts of warning, encouragement or of derision, especially when the film or the projector breaks down. When it does it is a chance to let off steam. We whistle, and there are cries of 'Come on' to encourage the operator. Discipline is relaxed, and everyone enjoys the change. My only memories of the programme are the serialised record of Sir Alan Cobham's pioneer flights to the Cape in 1925, and to Australia in 1926. All too soon the lights go on, the chairs are folded and stowed under the stage, and the supper cart is wheeled in. It is currant bread (currant toke), no margarine, one slice each. It has a peculiar musty taste, probably because it has been locked up in the cart all day.

We 'fall in' for the last time this day, and are marched to our various dormitories. We, of course, have to cross the parade to the far side, through No. 7 arches into the 'back yard' and up the fire-escape on which we take our boots off before entering the dormitory (see fig. 6).

The first thing one noticed on entering the dormitory was the floor ('the deck'). Polished to a finish that would be the envy of any cabinetmaker or french polisher, it was death to place a booted foot on it, far worse to walk on it with wet socks. I knew every knot in it personally before I left, but more of that later. It was a large, lofty room, with huge wooden beams and rafters on slender iron pillars supporting the roof (there was no ceiling). The walls were painted green up to about four feet from the floor, the remainder the usual buff colour. The windows were about half the size of those immediately below them on the first floor and were painted white.

In the main room there were about eighty beds in six long rows, the main gangway running between rows four and five. Halfway along on one side was the 'big square' with some twenty-one beds in seven rows, and the 'little square' at the

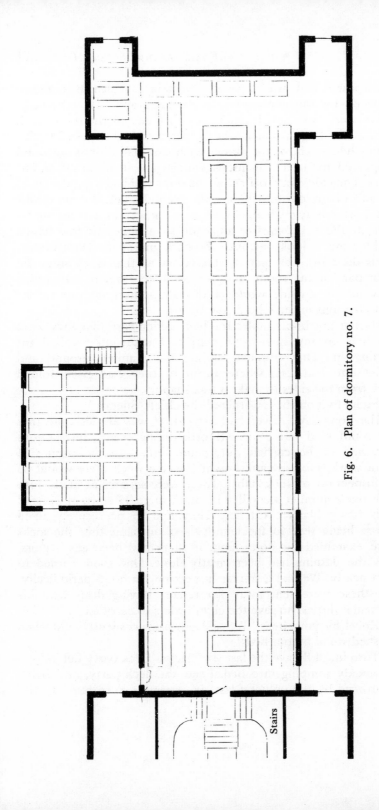

Fig. 6. Plan of dormitory no. 7.

Stairs

fire escape end was a small appendage which was almost
screened by the corners of the building and held four beds.
There were two 'stands', one at either end of the room, each
having four large wooden wheels which gave them some twelve
inches height above the floor. Each one had a brass surround
supported by iron stanchions which gave it an air of importance. The chief petty officer at the door end had a good view of
his half of the dormitory, and the second chief, the fire escape
end. Fortunately my bed, No. 84, was the second in from the far
wall in the little square, adjacent to a large window which
enabled me to look out onto the park and at the Observatory.
I was therefore well placed, able to see all that went on in the
main part of the room, and yet secluded from it with a nice
view of the outside world. I thought it must be one of the
best positions in the school (see fig. 6).

Placing my boots under the bed, taking care that they were
standing on my spread-out jumper, I made up my bed for
turning in. This entailed folding the blankets around and
under the mattress, where formerly they had been folded
back from the sides to make a box shape.

'Stand by your beds', ordered the chief. 'Silence.'

The company officer had arrived. It was at this time that
he would read out items of forthcoming events, instructions
that had to be carried out, complaints, and the issuing of
extra work, etc., as punishment. Once a week there would be
an inspection of sock 'tabs'. These were squares of duck-cloth
with one's number stencilled in, and a large 'H' sewn in worsted
with fancy blanket stitches. They had to be securely fixed
before being sent to the laundry. At the same time the socks
were examined for holes, and, if there had been any repairs,
that the darning had been neatly done. One soon learned to
darn neatly. We had a similar inspection for boots periodically,
but these were sent away for repair. Having dealt with his
particular duties, he gave the chief orders to carry on.

'Kneel by your beds.' We said our prayers silently, and when
finished stood by our beds.

'Turn in.' 'I'll have the last six.' Then, 'Deck party fall in.'

Quickly jumping into bed, I saw the deck party, now being
reinforced by the unlucky last six, assemble in front of the fire

16. The first 'Fame'.

17.   The second 'Fame' about 1865.

18. The 'Fame' showing figurehead, 1890.

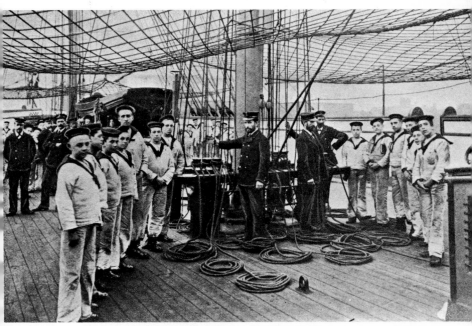

19. On board 'Fame' about 1890.

20.   Ship under full sail, 1890.

21.   Manning the yards, 1890.

escape, collecting their polishing clothes ('deckies') on the way. Forming into three rows, they knelt down, and awaited the order to scrub ('polish').

Scrubbing decks was an exercise which, although not achieving the maximum polishing results, gave the most discomfort to the polisher, and leant itself to the greatest measure of discipline. Kneeling as upright as possible, with back straight, head up and looking to the front; the arms were extended as far to the left as possible. The cloth doubled into a rectangle was held down firmly with all one's weight on both hands which were placed together, palms down. On the order the arms were swung smartly across the shortest distance from left to right in a short arc, then back to the left, and so on the command of the P.O. in charge.

'Left, right. Lef., righ.' 'Ease . . . back.' Smartly they marched backwards, knees and arms in step. 'Ease . . . forward.' Forward they moved to their original positions. 'Ease . . . left.' 'Lef. Righ. Lef. Righ. Lef. . . . Lef. . . . Lef. . . . Lef. Righ. Lef. . . .'

Backwards and forwards they moved, left and right, down between the beds to the door end, back along the next corridor, until the hour was up and they were allowed to turn-in to bed. I found the most trying part of this punishment was the many knots protruding from the floor which soon made one's knees tender. It took me some six months before I invented and made a pair of knee-pads that were strapped to the knees, under the trousers of course, before operations. I wonder if I was the only one who thought of this idea? When scrubbing between the rows of beds and when the P.O. was not looking, one could just go through the motions by thumping the floor with the hands, and bobbing one's head up and down, thereby having a little breather. While the deck party were performing their evolutions, the remainder of us were reading, writing letters, or just dozing off. This last hour of the day was very pleasant to me, especially in the summer. The noises from the people in the park below, the fresh smell of the grass and trees that came in the window. As the daylight faded, tired, and in the only place where one could really relax, one fell asleep.

I had learnt that life was now continuously controlled by a succession of bugle calls and other orders given not so much by the company officers, but by the boy officers. These were the chief, the second chief, four or five first-class petty officers, and six or so second-class petty officers. These, armed with rope-ends suitably embellished with fancy knots, or strips of leather spliced into small but painful weapons, called 'stonicky', chivvied one along at each command. This invariably included taking the numbers of the last six or last three, these unfortunates being the candidates for the deck party that evening. All the boy officers wore leather slippers ('nimbles') in the dormitory, and these were the favourite weapons used on the deck parties, or during the normal daytime working periods. They could either be thrown at an unsuspecting victim's face, or delivered by hand behind the neck, and there were many other variations, all of them unpleasant. The most common form of movement on command was the 'double', but for any very long distances we usually marched, although any sign of slackness when marching brought the order to double.

The boys themselves came from many walks of life, the youngest, usually from some orphan home, such as Swanley, that catered for children up to 10 years of age. There were some who, one parent having died, the other re-married, decided that their son would be better off at a school away from home. Others, many of them whose fathers themselves were 'Old Boys', were there because of the excellent schooling available, both academic as well as in seamanship. It was difficult to tell the ratio between the orphans and the more fortunate ones, but as I had been born in the first months of World War I, it seems obvious that during my period at the school there was a very high proportion of fatherless boys.

Chapter Four

THE FIRST WEEK

THE REVEILLE SOUNDS, it is six o'clock, the company officer calls out 'Wakey, wakey, rise and shine', as he walks up the main gangway of the dormitory. He turns up the dimmed gaslamps and we start another day. There is no time to think as we turn out and dress (later I learn to get out of, or get into, underpants, trousers and socks in one swift operation), strip the bed, pick up my boots and bolt for the fire-escape door. Already the P.O.s are there giving a tap here and there with the rope's end, and waiting to take the numbers of the last few. Fortunately, my bed is quite near the door, and I am soon wedged in the solid mass going down the stone steps. The cold and damp wind blows through my shirt and I shiver as I hastily slip on my boots on the way down; there is no time to lace them. It is very dark, the ground is uneven and the route is unfamiliar, and I stumble on towards the wash lavatory. After a wash that finally awakens me, I continue with the stampede back to the dormitory. I endeavour to make up my bed as quickly and as neatly as my next-door neighbour, No. 83, who finds time to give me some help.

The beds were, unlike those at Trafalgar Quarters, really made-up neatly. The counterpanes had the school crest in the centre and a cable-pattern border running about twelve inches from the edge with an anchor in each corner. The bedclothes were tucked in under the mattress, hospital fashion, to form a box. On special occasions we would bite along the cable pattern border top to make a really sharp edge. (A new mattress, although comfortable to sleep on, was a great disadvantage towards this end, as it was almost impossible to get nice sharp edges and corners.)

My bed finally finished, I report to the second chief for duty and I am told to do a bit of dusting around for the time being.

55

Soon 'cooks' is sounded, and these lucky ones go to prepare breakfast and get the largest portions that they can safely serve themselves. About ten minutes later we are assembled and marched over to the gym, and soon after we arrive the 'fall in' routine is repeated, and so to breakfast. In addition to the usual bread ration and 'dip' of ship's cocoa (with a liberal amount of fat swimming about on the surface) we have a little extra for breakfast. Kippers one day, minced meat ('tollage') the next, corned beef, salmon, luncheon sausage, herrings, are all I can remember. Later on, I found that by putting the aluminium plate on top of the hot cocoa I could melt the 'dripping' out of the corned beef, thereby augmenting my margarine ration; it also made the meal more palatable as I disliked too much fat. After breakfast it is back to work in the dormitory where I am told to help with one of the rows. There is a boy detailed off to each row of beds, and it is up to him to see that it passes the close scrutiny of the company officer at the end of the work period. We commence by tying a floor cloth round the head of the broom (to collect the fluff) and sweep the dust and fluff from under the beds into the gangway. We then sweep the gangway from end to end.

The castors on the feet of the beds rested on wooden 'chocks' which were brought into line with the longitudinal joints of the floorboards until the beds were in a dead straight line. When this had been achieved, the boy on No. 1 row would sight across the headrails of the beds and point out any particular headrail that might be out of alignment and which had to be adjusted. By this means the beds were in line both ways.

The sheets were examined to make sure that the turn-down reached the painted mark on the side of the bed, thus ensuring that these also were in line. Last of all, the rolled-up nightshirts, each with the number showing, would be centred on the pillows so that they, too, would be in line from one end of the row to the other.

Each chock was now examined and any fluff removed, at the same time making sure there was no dust or fluff left on the floor. Then, starting at the end of the row, under the first bed, on one's back, one had to make sure that there were no corners or ends of bedclothes hanging down between the crossed iron slats ('dog's ears'). There were no springs to the beds. One drew oneself along by pulling on the legs of the beds, taking care not to disturb the alignment. One could be a long time at this job, and keep out of harm's way. A little dusting around the headrails, and it was soon time to be dismissed.

We make our way to the gymnasium; it is just after 8 a.m., and time to change into number twos, clean our boots, etc., and get ready for divisions. 'Fall in' sounds, and after the usual drill routine the company officer inspects us. A haircut ('crop') for one, another has dirty boots ('report to me in the dorm. tonight'). Eventually satisfied, he gives a smart salute as he reports to Lieutenant-Commander Yeo ('Yeo'y'), the chief officer.

The chaplain arrives, and from the stage conducts a short service, and just before nine o'clock the band, stationed near the door end, strikes up 'For wee'l make the keel row', and to this lively tune we double out, each boy to his task for the day. Some make their way to the classrooms, others to their various 'trades'. Trades was rather a misnomer, as it was only the tailors and the band who received training, and one remained in the same occupation for the whole of one's time at trades. The remainder were employed in the bakery, laundry, kitchen, and the various other 'shops', such as carpenter's shop, paint shop, etc., and on other jobs necessary for the running of the establishment, these jobs being changed around each term.

The school itself was divided into the 10 classes of Junior Division composed of boys up to thirteen and a half years of age, and the Senior Division of six classes of the older boys, who spent alternate days at school and trades, and the Advance Class, which was composed of the best boys from the Senior Division. The Upper Nautical was No. 9 company and to qualify to enter one had to pass a rather stringent educational examination, which was held before leaving Junior Division, usually when one was 13 years old. These boys were specially trained for the better branches of the Navy, artificers, etc.; the remainder of the school would go to Naval Training Establishments at Shotley, Portsmouth, or Plymouth as boy seamen and work their way up the promotion ladder from there. Their uniform differed slightly from ours. Instead of the sailor's jumper they wore 'monkey jackets' with two rows of brass buttons down the front. They also had gold badges and good-conduct stripes instead of the red worn by the remainder of the school. During this particular year they were the 'leading company'. This was the company judged to be the smartest during the previous year, and it entitled them to wear lanyards and to be the leading column, carrying the school banner when we were marching. There was also a company of Boreman Boys who attended the school daily and were attached to the Upper Nautical School. They did not attend our parades, and on the whole looked rather dowdy compared with their companions. They usually bore the brunt of any horse-play, snowballing, etc., and therefore usually made their way to the classrooms when we were at divisions, and made a prompt departure at the end of the day.

I eventually found myself ushered into class five (see plate 10). It was the normal kind of classroom, the main difference to my school at home was that the desks were now designed to contain all one's books, and the blackboard, instead of being on an easel, was in a frame which in turn was mounted on castors. The buff-coloured paper and exercise books seemed rather cheap.

Our master, P.D. Rice (all masters were known as P.D.s., punishment deliverers) was a very thin man, his dark suit and hard collar fitting loosely around a frail frame. From time to time he would go to the cupboard behind the blackboard and mix a drink of Glaxo, much to the boys' delight, although they took good care not to be caught misbehaving. The main thing that fascinated me was his Adam's apple. When he swallowed, it appeared to travel several inches. It could be during a history lesson, 'Now we will deal with The Divine Right of Kings', he would say. The apple would ascend from nadir to zenith and return, like the ball on the Observatory mast at noon. So the lesson would progress, the interest in the Stuarts and the neck being about equal, until he would say, 'Now turn to page twenty-one and copy chapter three'. There would be a rustling of books and paper, and from behind the blackboard a clink of glass.

Soon 'defaulters' sounds, followed some minutes after by 'stand easy'. We file out for a break. Running round to the parade I view the squad lined up outside the office, awaiting 'trial', and to speculate on what punishment they were going to receive. Up to three strokes with the cane for minor cases can be awarded from 'Yeo'y', and for the more serious cases the offenders are bound-over to report to 'skipper's defaulters' and are then marched to the Queen's House to go before the admiral, who can give a sentence of six or nine strokes with a large cane. This is carried out in No. 9 dormitory, where two gymnasium instructors hold the victim over a bed during the punishment. In very bad cases, fortunately not very often, a boy would be expelled.

Apart from learning the first chapters of 'The Acts of the Apostles' and wondering why we should have to worry about learning John Gilpin's famous ride, I don't remember much about this class. I don't recall the stick being used, so it must have been a rather happy time. P.D. Rice, for all his ill health, must have been a good master, because when I left his tuition, it was to class three that I went instead of class four.

The rest of the morning passes and we are dismissed for our midday meal. 'Cooks' is soon sounded; afterwards the 'fall in'. The usual rush to the dining hall, and more leisurely trot out again, and for some, the highlight of the day, letters. Our company officer would be outside No. 7 wash lavatory, and when a suitable number of boys had collected, would call out the numbers and distribute letters to the lucky ones. He would also have a list of parcels awaiting collection at the parcels office near the gate.

About ten minutes to one, the 'fall in' sounds, but this time it is for 'skirmish'. Our company forms a line from No. 7 wash lavatory to the outside railings. Other companies form up at different stations around the parade so that when we march forward the whole area is covered. After we have positioned ourselves at arm's length apart, the signal is given and we all move forward, picking up any pieces of paper, etc., that lie in our paths. Our particular area stretched from the line I have already given to the northern extremity of the parade, and was entirely covered with shingle. After I had been at the school for some time, I always chose the position nearest to the railings. Although there was more rubbish to be picked up from among the bushes, it was nice to be near the outside world and, if no one was looking, pass the time of day with any young lady who might be passing. After depositing our collection at the dust hole we made our way towards our various daily activities, a bugle-call hastening us on our way.

The rest of the afternoon passed, and after tea and our evening wash it was time for nightschool and seamanship classes. My evenings for nightschool were to be Tuesdays and Fridays, and my seamanship class Thursdays. We started at six o'clock and finished at seven. The seamanship class held in the evening took place in one of the classrooms. Although there was a proper room fitted out with working models and life-size ship's equipment, this was too advanced for us beginners and was used for the day pupils only. The subject for us this term was Flags and Pendants used in Naval Signalling. I noted with some degree of envy the notebooks produced by my classmates showing the neatly-coloured flags with their descriptions and meanings written underneath. I resolved that at the first opportunity I would buy some crayons and a notebook. The lesson was very interesting. A company officer took the class, and using little wooden flags with metal eyes, so that they could be hung from hooks on small masts each some three feet high and from yard arms, signals were made from one 'ship' to the other. The various manoeuvres that resulted from these activities were explained in some detail on the blackboard. We sailed in line-ahead, line-abreast; ships were ordered, 'away sea-boat's crew', and the flagship called on various ships to perform different types of evolutions and in all we spent a very interesting evening.

The highlight of the next day, Friday, is the march past (see plate 26). 'Fall in' sounds at about a quarter to twelve, and the whole school assembles on the parade ground. Each company is formed into two ranks facing the colonnade, with No. 9 company in front, No. 1 behind, and so on, my company being in line with the office. The tallest boys are at each end of the columns, the shortest in the centre—I am somewhere in between.

There is the usual routine of forming fours, back into two deep, and lining-up by the right to get into straight lines. The band which forms in six files, with the drum-major in front, is to our left, halfway along the ship, facing us. Eventually the last company officer reports to 'Yeo'y', and when he is satisfied that all is ready he nods to the bandmaster. There are two, three-paced rolls on the drums. The band strikes up a lively march and the leading company moves off. They wheel left and march towards the space between the stern of the ship and the Queen's House, followed by the remaining companies. In the meantime, the band has turned left and taken up position ahead of the leading company as they march past to salute the admiral. Soon it is our turn; 'Eyes right', the chief petty officer salutes the admiral, who from the balcony salutes in return. 'Eyes front'—one's body tingles with excitement with the band playing—the orders being obeyed as one. We march around the parade to our original positions and are dismissed. 'Cooks' is sounded, and I await impatiently for dinner, which on Friday is fried fish for half the school, and salmon for the remainder; the latter was always spoilt for me by the sauce with which it was covered.

In the dormitory that night we are detailed for our various 'stations' for the following morning. I have to report to the laundry. Reveille sounds at five-thirty, and after the usual scramble to wash, we return to make up our beds for inspection. Sheets, blankets and counterpane are folded in a special manner, presenting a neat pile at the head of the bed. Pillow case, handkerchief, and our complete clean change of under-wear are arranged, each with the number showing, along the length of the bed.

All the beds in the main part of the dormitory are now pushed to the sides, and a row of boys spreads a layer of thick polish over the cleared section of the floor, the remainder of the lads getting down to polish. This is my first experience of scrubbing, and after a very short time I realise what exhausting work it is. Backwards and forwards we go, keeping up the regular rhythm to the petty officers' chant of 'Left, right', etc., while they move along the rows seeking any one slacking. The polish mixed with turpentine soon soaks through the knees of my trousers, and as I swing my arms from side to side, my knees slide on the rough canvas insides. The effect of the polish, knots in the floor and the rough trousers soon makes my knees sore, and I pray for the time when we can get to breakfast. We have a few short rests during the hour of hard labour, and eventually we replace the beds, cooks having previously left. We at last fall-out for breakfast.

The laundry, a long, narrow building sited along the eastern walls was really Dickensian—the arched cast-iron framed windows, the painted brick wall on which was fastened the shaft and whirling wheels driving the belt-driven machines. Washing-machines rotated, slopping, frothy, soapy water all over the floor. Wooden trolleys loaded with soaking washing were being pushed about by clog-footed boys from one machine to another. We made our way through the noise and steam into the ironing room where a huge steaming roller was rotating. It was my job, with another two boys, to feed sheets into this monster, and at the other side the hot sheets were folded and stacked into piles ready for sorting. I had a really good billet as the remaining half dozen of the squad spent the next two and a half hours scrubbing the huge wooden floors of the sorting room, with scrubbing brushes each nearly the size of a broom head. Towards the end of the morning there was a chance for some fun. Now that the floor was dry, we were able to walk about on it in our stockinged feet, and as the trolley-loads of clean clothes, still warm from the drying room, arrived and were dumped in heaps on the floor, we dived into the warm mass, burying one another and having a fine old skylark.

The whole of one side of the wall in the sorting room was occupied by large racks or bins, each marked with a company letter and number, including the infirmary, Trafalgar quarters, kitchen, etc. We soon got to work sorting out the ever-increasing pile of shirts, socks and all the various items, throwing them into 'H' for Howe, 'C' for Collingwood as the case might be, taking care to aim a few at one another occasionally to keep things lively. At last our labours came to an end, and I made my way across the parade thinking of the dinner to come as I felt ravenously hungry.

I was agreeably surprised to find that my acquaintance at Trafalgar quarters, Jack, was seated at the next mess table, but on the far side. After several attempts at turning completely round without drawing too much attention to myself, I signalled that I would meet him on the way out. We met outside the gym and decided to spend the afternoon putting 'cheese cutters' in our trousers, which were issued with creases on the sides, as opposed to the front and back of civvies. What we had to do was to reverse these side creases from pointing outwards to inwards. This seemingly impossible task, without the aid of a hot iron, was achieved by turning the trousers inside-out, and biting along the creases until they were obliterated. This unsavoury, jaw-aching task continued throughout the afternoon in the semi-quiet of the arches, until the four creases, wet with saliva, were showing some signs of improvement. After tightly rolling the trousers (a part of the pressing process) they were carefully stowed away in our lockers. We exchanged our experiences to date, and how we found our new mode of life. Jack, who unlike myself, had been eager to join the school, was really disillusioned. With hair cropped like a convict, dressed in an ill-fitting, misshapen suit made of canvas cloth soiled with the marks of recent labours; his trousers trussed-up at the waist by a heavy webbed belt, and on his feet, a pair of heavy military-type boots, which were to defy any attempts to get them to shine for weeks; this certainly was not the rig to go swaggering around Bristol.

On Sunday morning we had the pleasure of a lie-in for an extra half-hour and that was not all, for it cut down the working time between make up of beds and breakfast. We made up our beds 'for Sunday', that is with the better side of the counterpane uppermost, and, if possible, a still neater finish. After breakfast we completed our various working tasks and, after we were dismissed, prepared for 'divisions'.

Boots are carefully polished (in my case hopelessly). 'No. 1' suits are carefully unrolled and donned, freshly laundered collars are squared up and silks folded. (This black silk was about one yard square, and at a later date would be soaked with water, folded first in halves from corner to corner forming a triangle, and then continued to fold until it was about one and a half inches wide and some four feet long. A knot was formed about six inches from each end to retain the folds, and it was then placed between the mattress and lower blanket so that it would be pressed as flat as possible.) It is supposed that these are worn to commemorate the death of Nelson, but it is probably a relic of the days when seamen wore a bandana round their head when in action to prevent their hair and sweat getting into their eyes. Caps are brushed, and everything tidied up to look as smart as possible.

'Fall in' sounds, there is a rush to the parade ground, and we line up in companies as before. There are the usual formalities of 'Dress to the right', 'Number', 'Form fours', 'Form two deep', and so on.

At last all is ready, the company officer is satisfied that all is in order and reports to Chief Officer Yeo, and returns; we are then stood at ease. The band starts playing. It is pleasant music—a waltz—'Waters of the Danube', 'Over the Waves', or something similar. The sun shines. Rear-Admiral Oliphant and the Surgeon Captain descend the steps from the Queen's House and make their way towards the first column. When they arrive, Yeo, who has been waiting at the head of the columns, salutes and falls in behind the doctor, accompanied by the C.O. of No. 9 and the boy C.P.O. who has already called the company to attention, and the 'inspection' proceeds. Eventually they reach our company and are met by Mr. B. and our C.P.O., who, calling us to attention, salute, and both fall in behind the chief officer.

We spring smartly to attention. My heart beats faster. It is the first time I have seen an admiral in the flesh. He looks dignified, rather pale faced, thoughtful; he occasionally leans a little on his silver-mounted cane. The doctor, slightly bent at the shoulders, says something. I notice the red bands between the gold rings on his sleeve. The admiral nods; they pass on.

'Front rank, one pace forward . . . March'. They progressed between the two ranks of our company. 'Front rank, one pace back . . . march'. The small procession soon moves down the ranks of No. 8 company and then back to the Queen's House. The Admiral nods, Yeo salutes, we are dismissed and disperse into small groups.

Very shortly afterwards the 'fall in' sounds, and we reassemble, but this time the band is at the rear, nearest to the gate. We go through the usual drill of forming fours, and when all is ready, the band strikes up a stirring march and moves towards the gate, followed by each company in turn. I notice that the band, after crossing Rodney Road, marches up the wide path between the two large buildings of the college and halts, while the rest, immediately they have passed the college gates, wheel to the right and march under the colonnade and into the chapel. Soon it is our turn to cross the road. There is quite a large crowd gathered to see the scene. Queues of trams and cars block the road as far as I can see; the people crowd around the gates and line along the railings to get a good view. As I cross the road the proximity of the spectators, the thought of being outside the school, the exhilarating martial music, all make my heart beat fast with excitement, and for a brief moment it feels that this really is the life (see plate 39).

We enter the chapel and, passing along the side passage, take our seats. (We were not allowed to walk on the centre aisle, which, paved in black and white marble in 1789, was too valuable to be subjected to our heavy boots.) Our company's seats were on the right or starboard side of the aisle, from about the fifth pew from the front, No. 9 company occupying the first few rows on our side. I looked around at the rather small pews which through the years had been liberally decorated by the idle occupants carving their numbers on the narrow shelves on the backs of the pews, which should be used exclusively for prayer and hymn books.

The magnificence of the place filled me with awe. The richly decorated ceiling painted in light blue and gold, below which on either side, were galleries, where the naval officers'* uniforms with their gold braid seemed to form a setting for the sprinkling of coloured dresses of the ladies who accompanied them. In front, the huge brass lectern stood beside the richly-carved pulpit, which stood on the other side of the aisle from where it now stands. The latter on its six fluted columns and the graceful curved staircase then looked, and still

*These officers were from the college.

does, a masterpiece of workmanship, some say by a Richard Lawrence of the old Deptford dockyard. At the back, above the altar, was a painting of St. Paul after the shipwreck on the isle of Malta. At the other end was the organ gallery over the doorway, supported on highly polished marble columns, with balusters surrounding the body of the organ, the pipes of which almost reached the ceiling. The stained glass windows (sadly these were destroyed by enemy action during World War II) completed the picture. The one thing that did strike me as odd, was that each choirboy wore a kind of sailor's collar around the neck of his surplice (see plate 5).

After the service we were marched back to the school where, after a short break, we went to dinner, the great attraction being baked potatoes which were a Sunday delicacy. There was another church service in the afternoon, and the rest of the day was ours. It was at this time that we donned our clean duck suits, which were to last until the following Sunday morning. My first job at this time was to write home.

It was at teatime on Sunday that cooks were detailed for the following week. There were port and starboard watches, and I was detailed either to the duty watch, which would be serving the following week, or to one that would finish that evening. Whichever one it was, I would continue in that watch as long as I remained in that particular mess. The boys at the top end of the table would get the choice numbers which would entail serving up the meals; the rest would go to our end, the worst of which was fifth cook. This job entailed washing the 17 knives and forks after each meal in sometimes almost cold water and, far worse, cleaning them after each midday meal except on Sundays. As they were made of ordinary steel, not stainless as they are today, they really needed cleaning each day, especially on a Monday or after we had vinegar or fish. The method used was to scrape some brick-dust off a sandstone brick on to a flat board one side of which was covered with leather, and briskly to rub first the handle, then the blade of the knife or the tines of the fork until they shone like silver. Obstinate cases needed treatment with the brick itself, but this was frowned upon as it left scratch marks on the metal. To be faced with 17 pairs of knives and forks, stained, and sometimes rusty, and to have them shining in about half an hour, was enough to daunt anyone. At the end of the cleaning session one had to report to the table on the square and have them examined where on the slightest pretext, such as a spot of brickdust between the tines of a fork, the whole lot would be rejected.

Sunday night was the time when the chief petty officer read out the 'stations' for the following week. It was during the 'announcement' period, just before we turned in. We all waited (that is the non-cooks) for our fate for the next seven days to be read out.

'Dom' (dormitory), he started, '3, 9, 17, 28', and so on. He read out the numbers of the boys for that particular duty. 'Lav.' (wash lavatory), '7, 19, 23', until the required number was reached. 'Windows', '14 and 33', only two boys being required on this job. 'Gym sweepers', and so it went on until everyone was detailed-off, and was either resigned to a week of unpleasant toil or elated at the prospects of an easy time.

Some of the jobs, not bad in themselves, were hated for different reasons. Dining hall sweeper, for instance, was quite an easy number, requiring the unfortunate only to sweep the central aisle from the far end to the central square. It did not take long, but it meant staying behind until all the cooks had finished after each meal. Scullery, on the other hand, was very hard and cold work. It entailed manning the 'spud machine' which was a cast-iron monster with an iron wheel on each side with a turning handle attached. A large funnel contraption at the top was filled with a bucket of potatoes and the two boys manning the handles turned like mad. The potatoes revolved around inside a central drum where they were scraped. When it was thought they were clean an iron handle was pulled down and they were ejected into a large trough of cold water.

I was once detailed to man the machine, and as bucket after bucket was endlessly poured into the machine, I fell exhausted on to the revolving handle and was thrown against the nearby wall. Fortunately, there was sufficient gap between the wall and the whirling handles for my crumpled body, or there may well have been a serious accident. After that episode

I was found a job at the trough, fishing the potatoes out of the cold water and filling the string net bags. We had to prepare enough for about one thousand boys, before eight o'clock, so no time could be lost.

'Dusthole' was a particularly good 'station.' There were two incinerator buildings, one at each end of the grounds. No. 7 dusthole was built close to the perimeter wall at the north-eastern corner, in our 'skirmish area'. Three boys, one from each of companies, Nos. 3, 6 and 7, manned this post and there was no direct supervision. The main task, apart from burning the rubbish, was toasting 'stungees', and there was a regular business carried on trading various small items or favours for this service. One of the 'cooks' on one's mess would 'look out' for one (see that you had a large portion each meal time), a loan of a pair of skates, a few sweets, or even a slice of the 'stungee' (this was the half-loaf ration cut into slices or sandwiches in such a way, that when they were placed together they fitted back so that sometimes it was difficult to see that the loaf had been cut at all) that one was toasting. There were a number of non-paying customers, P.O.s from each of the companies would send theirs, and sometimes their friends'. Sometimes the boiler got so hot that the bread could be toasted by just being placed on top, but most of the time one had to balance the slices on the rake and hold them over the hot embers. Such lucrative jobs were not given to 'new Jacks', and I was lucky to get this one.

'Stairs' was another good number, primarily because one was rewarded with a slice of cake from the company officer's wife at the end of the week. This job consisted of keeping the spiral stairs clean, from the top landing on either side leading to their bedrooms, down past the entrance to the dormitories, and then down past their front door to the next landing. These were stone steps with lead nosings, which had to be scrubbed and the lead polished. When they were scrubbed on Saturday, Mrs. B. would reward the lucky one with a slice of cake. The same reward went with a week at the Queen's House, with the additional attraction that it was a young servant girl who presented the gift.

My first station was probably 'fifth cook dom' which would entail washing the knives and forks in the morning and then reporting for odd jobs in the dormitory afterwards.

Monday morning, and school again. For dinner it would be corned beef and boiled potatoes covered with piccalilli. How I hated the latter: firstly I could not bear the taste of it, and secondly it turned the knives and forks black, and I had more than my share of cleaning them. Fortunately this was usually followed by baked apple pie, which was a great favourite. The four corners of the pastry were considered a special delicacy, and, consequently, were given to the four boys at the top of the table.

Twice a week while in Junior Division, and once a week in Senior, each class had to attend half an hour of physical training in the gymnasium. The instructors were still serving in the Navy, and their term of duty with us was only for a few months. They all appeared to me to have one thing in common—bad tempers. Invariably, as far as I can remember, the drill followed the same pattern. We would commence by forming into six ranks of six, six or seven feet from each other; the instructor would be on the stage. We would begin, perhaps with arms bending and stretching exercise, but within a very short time it would be, 'All right then, we want waking up', or words to that effect, and from then on it became more of a torture than training. There were several favourites. Running around the gym with one's arms upstretched can be very tiring.

'On to the lockers . . . Go.' There would be a scramble on to the top of the lockers.

'Fall in again.'

'On to the wallbars . . . Go.' We would climb up and perch like monkeys on the wallbars.

'Fall in again.' 'Double march . . . left wheel.' Round we would go again.

In the summer there was something special. We would double around, then proceed outside the gym to the fire escape from No. 2 dormitory. This, when it reached the level of the classrooms, divided into two separate stairways down to ground level, one opposite the other. The idea was to run up one side, across the small landing, and down the other, round to the first

Fig. 7.   The fire escape, dormitory no. 2.

stairs and up and over again. Very soon we were literally dragging ourselves up and down.

Hanging on the wallbars was less energetic but no less painful.
For this form of exercise we hung for long periods by the arms
from the top bar, and sometimes to add to our discomfort,
orders were given for 'arms bend'. This entailed heaving up and
lowering the whole weight of the body. Sometimes, when the
instructor was at the other end of the gym it was possible to
take the weight by standing on the lower bars with the backs
of the heels, but one needed to be the right height to be able
to appear hanging, and yet standing, and to pass unnoticed.
To be caught meant a session of lifting and lowering the legs
while still hanging, which very soon offset any rest one had
gained.

The highlight for Tuesdays was the march past. It was the
same procedure as for Fridays. When it was raining, instead of
march past, we assembled in the gymnasium for the hornpipe.
For this we formed into rows which stretched right across the
gym in the same formation as we would have done on the
parade. The band would strike up the hornpipe and we would
commence the first steps. 'Yeo'y' would be on the stage giving

instructions, sometimes giving us a demonstration of how it should be done by doing a few steps himself. There were two occasions during the dance when the right- and left-hand halves changed sides, and after a few sequences of steps, changed back again, the rule being that those moving from right to left went in front of those moving the other way. Sometimes there was some skylarking, some starting to move one way would quickly step forward or backward as the case may be, and join up with those moving the opposite way. Each company officer was stationed at the end of the rows, and 'Yeo'y' from his vantage point was not slow to pick out the offenders, but occasionally there were areas of chaos.

On Tuesdays it was Irish stew for dinner, a meal that was not very well liked; it may have come under the taboo of things considered not to be eaten. (There were several of these, although for what reason no one knew; it definitely wasn't because of any unpleasantness.) Cabbage (spinach), sausage meat (tollage) were immediately consigned to the waste bins, and anyone seen eating the forbidden items were classed as hogs and sometimes pelted with waste. Steamed currant pudding ('sloppy duff') was permitted, although to eat the soft top portion (the 'sloppy'), brought immediate retribution, and even eating the outside edges was frowned upon. It was therefore the mess shelf end that had the pleasure of the four corners of this pudding, and after a great show of cutting off the offending parts, and consigning them to the waste tin, it was a very small helping that was left.

On Wednesdays, if the weather was fine, we had a march out. Just before 11 a.m. we would be dismissed from our various tasks. The 'fall in' would sound and we would assemble on the parade ground as for church, the band being near the gate. There would be two three-pace rolls on the drums, the band would strike up, and we would form up in fours and march off. Out of the gate turning left into Romney Road, the band playing, the drum major swinging his mace into intricate patterns. The drum major, one· of the smaller boys, was dressed as a guardsman, complete with bearskin and sword. We turned to the left into King William Walk, passing the western boundary of the school where I had my first view of the infirmary from the outside. Then passing the old disused church (of course, said to be haunted), leaving the park gates on our left, we started to climb the steep slope of Coomb Hill, the bushes of the park showing through the railings on our left. The band now stopped playing and we were marching to a regular tap on the side drum. At the top of the hill we followed the wall of the park, turning to the left and along the straight stretch of Charlton Way. The band struck up again, this time it was the bugle and side drum section, which sounded rather brassy after the full band. Blackheath Common stretched away to our right, and about halfway along this section of the road, on our left, were the huge cast-iron gates of the southern entrance to the park. As we approached the far corner, the order came 'Eyes left'. The company officers and chiefs saluted as we paid our respects at the newly-erected war memorial to the 1914-18 dead. Descending Maze Hill, still keeping to the perimeter of the park, I was beginning to feel tired. The drummer continued with his tap, tap, to keep us in step. As we turned at the end of this stretch I was relieved to see the school at the end of the road, but we had quite a way to go yet before we would get into Romney Road, and to the gate of the school. The brass band started again, and with the drum major swinging his mace, we marched briskly along the last half mile or so to the school.

It had been very pleasant to be in the outside world again, and our appetites, always hearty, were now sharpened by the fresh air and exercise. For dinner on Wednesdays it was beef, or mutton, boiled potatoes and cabbage, with perhaps rice or prunes and custard to follow. In the afternoon it was 'make and mend' or half-day, and so I concluded my first week at the school, a routine which basically did not alter from one year to another.

Chapter Five

TOWARDS END OF TERM

THE FOLLOWING SATURDAY was 5 November, and after our evening wash we gathered around the sides of the parade ground to see the firework display. It was a cold dark night, and I positioned myself in one of the arches near the office. The display lasted for about an hour, and there were fireworks going off from several different areas at the same time. Rockets were sent up from all parts of the ship, and there was a general scramble to collect any sticks that may have fallen within reach of the crowd. What use they could be put to when found and successfully fought for is anyone's guess. Jumping crackers were tossed into the audience, and were kicked around, causing a rare old disturbance; catherine wheels, too, were allowed to roll along the ground towards the spectators. In the light of the flashes, and from the vocal response, it was apparent that a large crowd had gathered and was watching the scene from outside the railings. It was the largest and longest display I had ever seen and it made a very pleasant evening. As we dispersed 'supper' sounded and I made my way (no doubt with my friend Jack) to the gym to collect my three 'doggies' (ship's biscuits).

About three weeks later I had a pleasant surprise. The company officer made his usual appearance in the dormitory, and at the appropriate time the order came, 'Stand by your beds.' 'Now it is only four weeks before we start our Christmas leave, and I want all boys who are travelling to write home for the money for the necessary fares. I must have it by the 14th December: Portsmouth, 7s. 2d., Plymouth . . .', and so he named the various main towns and the fares required. 'Leave'—the very word thrilled me as I tumbled into bed. What had been a far-off dream, too far away to consider seriously, was now becoming a reality, and was being prepared

73

for. My next letter home would contain the magic words, 'I shall be coming home on leave on 21 December, can you send the fare, 7s. 2d., as soon as possible?' Where would my mother get the money? This was an uncertainty which did not bear thinking about; I was sure that somehow the money would arrive, as it did in due course.

During the last few weeks some of the boys had been preparing for the fancy dress ball. Of course everything was done in the strictest secrecy, for two reasons. Firstly, it was unwise to let anyone know what you were going to do, as prizes were awarded and ideas could be improved on, so it was wise to keep ideas and materials to oneself. Secondly, the method of obtaining the necessary pieces of material sometimes did not bear too close an investigation.

The Saturday night arrived. The band took up its position on the flag-decked stage. Bunting (old flags) were draped here and there, and this gave the gym a gala appearance. There were numerous pirates complete with black patch over one eye and handkerchiefs tied round the head although, goodness knows, there was little enough hair to be kept out of the eyes. Sailors of Nelson's day were depicted by striped jerseys, which told of discreet visits to Nurse Tock's shop where the school's linen was repaired, and a subsequent raid of the company's boot blacking tin. In both cases wooden cutlasses were worn. Discarded blue suits, which could be wheedled out of the master tailor at the tailors' shop for such an occasion, were re-designed as all kinds of garments, and even the humble deck cloths came in for castaways' attire. Pieces of bunting were used with amazing results, while rope ends combed out into fine strands made long hair and beards.

The visitors arrived. Company officers' wives, parents of boys who lived locally, gamely bringing daughters with them, added lustre to the scene. Unfortunately, there were not many girls brave enough to accept the offers of the heavily-shod gallants who offered to partner them. Foxtrot followed waltz, and then perhaps a one-step, always a favourite as all one had to do was to march around. 'Yeo'y' in his number ones was in his element on the stage directing operations, especially during the Lancers, when we were expected to put on a good show.

Admiral danced with convict as they bowed partners and swung corners or did the grand chain. As the evening drew to a close the fancy-dressed competitors paraded across the stage and three were selected as the best and stood in the centre of the stage to collect their prizes. The first prize, for two years running, was won by 'John Bull', complete with top hat, Union Jack waistcoat, and of all things, a live bulldog. Where he obtained the latter was a complete mystery to me; he might have been a local whose family pet dog came in for the occasion, or one of the staff might have loaned it to the boy. I never did find out, but it was the climax to a very merry evening.

The following week we had the Assault at Arms. The chairs were prepared in the gym and after our evening visit to the wash lavatory we seated ourselves as if we were going to watch a film, the exception being that the two front rows were occupied by the admiral, doctor, 'Yeo'y' and other officers and some of their families. For the next hour and a half we watched various gymnastic displays by boys who had been selected as the best and spent hours in practice to reach the high standards shown.

Vaulting over the horse, parallel bars, and club swinging were all carried out with precision, with loud applause after each act. The club swinging in the dark was very effective. An electric light bulb was attached to each club and the lights were dimmed (this took some time as it was all gas lighting at the school), the subsequent light-patterns gained rounds of applause. In the final act all the participants formed a huge tableau, the top of which stood five high from the floor. There was no music at all that evening, so at the end it was a rather silent departure as we collected and stowed the chairs followed by bread-and-cheese supper.

The last Friday of the term was known as Cadders Eve. The theory was that if you had broken off a friendship during the term and not made it up by this time, now was the time to do so, failing which the protagonist had to be found and his face smeared with boot polish. This sounds harmless enough, but sometimes it resulted in gangs of about forty boys looking for trouble. On one occasion I was chased by one of these mobs and I fortunately managed to seek refuge at the top of a fire escape. Whether I was their intended victim or it was a case of mistaken identity, I did not waste time to find out. On a later occasion my friend Jack ended up in the infirmary, about which I will write later. On this occasion, however, things were uneventful as far as I was concerned. Jack and I had by now become firm friends, but because he was in a different company, No. 6, and in a different class at school, we did not spend much time in each other's company.

Walking Sunday, the last Sunday in the term, was observed by disobeying all orders to double. Why this should be, I never could find out. It would commence when we assembled for breakfast in the gym. On the order 'double march, right wheel', the response would be simply to walk. The C.P.O. would place himself at the end of the ranks prior to giving the order, so that he could emphasise its meaning by repeating it and at the same time giving the nearest unfortunate a shove. But it was all to no purpose, the more timid ones would shuffle a few paces and then fall in with the rest.

At church that afternoon the end of term hymn 'Lord Dismiss us with Thy Blessing' was sung with gusto, but I could not help noticing with a chilly feeling that the next one in the book was 'Lord Receive us with Thy Blessing' and that when we sang it, there would be a long full term to serve. Around the school at this time could be heard the following song, which was repeated on the next two days with the necessary alteration of the first line.

> In three days' time where shall I be,
> Outside this place of misery,
> No more P.O.s to order us about,
> No more C.O.s to shout 'Turn out'
> And happy I shall be,
> With the baby on my knee,
> Singing the melody,
> Of Home Sweet Home.
> No more spinnage for me,
> No more brick dust in tea,
> No more tollage for breakfast,
> That is the life for me.

Haversacks had been placed on each bed, and as each item of linen arrived back from the laundry, it was neatly rolled and stowed away ready for packing. The Tuesday before leave was Leave Cash Day. In the morning it was Saturday routine, and we were employed until noon on our various cleaning tasks. After dinner and skirmish, there was a general move towards the gym. Trestle tables had been laid out above which boards bore the names of the main railway stations for which tickets could be bought. Already long lines had gathered at the Portsmouth, Plymouth, and Chatham tables. Before queuing for tickets, however, cash had to be collected at the appropriate table. By the time I had collected my money, the Portsmouth queue had diminished in length, and after a short wait, I collected my ticket and stowed it safely in my belt pocket.

It was the unwritten law that the greater part of the afternoon should be spent polishing boots. Some were fortunate enough to have them old and mature, polished, boned and polished again until a mirror finish was obtained. We each had two pairs, the better of which were known as the leave pair. A certain amount of planning had to be done to ensure that one had the right pair at the right time. This sometimes required the expedient of knocking off the steel protector that was fastened around the bottom of the heel, and sending them to repair early in the term, and if necessary repeating the process in time for the leave period. But the job had to be done properly if one was to avoid a cuff round the ear when they were inspected. Jack and I settled down in one of the arched recesses at the base of the junior classroom block (all the recesses on either side of this block were fitted with wooden seats) armed with brushes, toothbrush handle, polishing cloth and some 'Cherry Blossom' polish which Jack supplied. We repeated the sequence of polish, bone, shine, bone and shine, time and time again, until we had a faint glimmer of success at last.

All was excitement in the dormitory that evening. The haversacks were now packed with number two blue suits, a change of underclothes, collar and socks, our number ones, nearly folded, and placed under the bed, all ready to don the following morning. Our company officer had brought his large horned gramophone which stood on a table just outside the Big Square, and we had a rendering of 'Old Comrades', 'Colonel Bogey' and other marches. Talking within reason was allowed. For myself, I waited impatiently for 'lights out', the unaccustomed noise got on my nerves and I wanted to get to sleep to bridge the remaining hours before the time of departure.

We were awakened early the next morning. There was no encouragement or threat needed to clear the dorm. as we rushed down to wash; and on return, beds were made in record time. As soon as this had been completed, cooks were away, followed by a general exodus from the dorm., and a rush to the gym to 'fall in' for breakfast. It was always luncheon sausage for breakfast on leave mornings. There were some who made a great show of not eating anything but, knowing that it would be at least another five hours before I had another meal and as it was one of my favourites, I devoured mine with great relish. All the boys who had long distances to travel were issued with Cornish pasties ('tiddey oggies'), and there was a certain amount of trading done with these. I often wondered how those who sold them for a few coppers fared on their long journeys, some having to go as far as Scotland or Cornwall.

The 'fall in' sounds for the last time this term, and most of the boys are there already. It is still dark. We don't waste much time going through the forming fours drill, just enough to get formed up. The band strikes up and we roar with cheers as we move off. As we march down the road, we can hear what the band is playing: it is 'Home Sweet Home'; there are more cheers, and the early morning silence is rent as eight hundred or so throats bawl out the words. There is a change of tune, 'Marching down to Georgia'; we join in with our own words:

> Goodbye Greenwich, goodbye spinnage,
> Goodbye Greenwich, we're gone forever more.

The journey to Waterloo Junction is uneventful, but when we arrive we spill out onto the platform, rush up along the covered corridor, across York Road and into Waterloo station. As soon as we get to the ticket barrier on the departure platform there is a general rush for the cigarette machines and kiosks. There is a special train laid on for us, and we are soon aboard and seated; within a very short time, amid thunderous cheers, we move off.

We have hardly left the station when cigarettes are lit and passed round. Soon each compartment resembles a tailor's shop. Jumpers are taken off, and the business of sewing up the sides of the body and sleeves to make a skintight fit, so necessary in a 'tiddly' suit. The short tapes, or 'fancies', used to tie the silk at the bottom of the vee of the jumper, are removed and substituted by others about twelve inches long. New badges, not always what the owner is entitled to (called 'fudging') I am afraid replace the old. Lanyards are produced, and moving the bow of the cap ribbon so that it is over the left eye instead of the left ear completes the picture.

As the train passes Havant and steams along the marshland of Bedhampton towards Portsmouth, heads begin to crowd round the open windows. When we near the bridge over Portsmouth Creek, we all begin to chant 'Into, into, into . . .' and as we cross, 'Pompey! Hurrah!' Cheers ring out all along the train and continue all the way to Fratton station, and after a brief stop for passengers to disembark, the town station.

At last we arrive, and I am delighted to see my mother, brother and sister waiting for me. Soon I am home again; my dear grandma, bursting into tears, retires to the kitchen, and grandfather tries to hide his feelings of emotion. How small everything seems, small houses, small rooms; there is hardly enough room to move around.

Chapter Six

THE START OF A NEW TERM

THE SIXTEEN DAYS LEAVE passed all too quickly, and soon the time came to depart. At the station the train arrived at the high level and we scrambled aboard. To many it was like a Sunday school outing, some skylarking, others contesting for corner seats. It was all good fun, with much waving and shouts of 'goodbye'. I found a vacant seat and sat there, glumly looking on as we pulled away from the station and sped non-stop past Fratton on our return journey. As we passed through the gorse-covered downlands and hazel thickets between Petersfield and Guildford the carefully-tailored jumpers were altered back to their original shapes, and as we clickety-clicked our way past Clapham Junction and arrived at Waterloo we were all subdued and properly dressed.

It was strange walking through the streets of Greenwich where I had previously marched under supervision. I was still at liberty, but as I walked along outside the railings of the school towards the gates it was with a feeling that a curtain was being slowly dropped, separating me from the outside world.

We always returned from leave on a Friday and by the time we had finished our work on Saturday morning we were almost back into the usual routine. In the afternoon Jack and I would spend part of the afternoon under the stern of the ship in the space formed between the rudder, which was hard over to starboard, and the shipside. There we would share out the good things we had brought back with us. The way things were shared was very simple. When two or more boys were to share anything, the idea was to be first in calling out 'Bore have first pick' ('I want first choice'), the second, 'Second pick', and so on. If there were only two sharing, then the one who had lost the choice would divide or break the cake or bar, the other

80

would choose his piece; then the other would do the dividing and so on. No scales or even balances would be needed for the accuracy of the shares, and it was guaranteed training for hand and eye.

I had, during the past weeks, given some considerable thought to the problem of raising the money for my fare home, and it was when I was writing home on the Sunday that I partly found the answer. While on leave I was proudly taken to my two great-aunts, that is, my grandfather's sister, who lived at Gosport, and my grandmother's sister, who resided locally, to let them see the latest acquisition to Britain's naval might. Both had placed a sixpenny-piece in my hand. It was therefore only common courtesy for me to inform them of my safe return, and again thank them for their generosity. For good measure I also wrote to my paternal grandmother who lived in one of the remoter districts of Shropshire, telling her of my new style of life and my new address. Sure enough, in due course, I received three letters in reply, each bearing a one shilling postal order. This, indeed, was a good venture, nearly half the fare at one go. I therefore decided that another letter of thanks would be sent about three weeks before the end of term, thanking them for their kindness and drawing attention to the nearness of the forthcoming leave, which in turn indeed gave the same result. From then on I always managed to save enough money to repay my mother my train fare on my return home.

During spring term the emphasis was on boxing and, although the new boys were not expected to take a very active part, we were taught the basic punches and defence during our physical training periods. Unfortunately, I only learned the use of the 'Left lead to jaw'. This consists of lunging at the opponent's jaw with the left fist, at the same time stepping forward with the left foot, while protecting one's own jaw by covering it with the right-hand glove. This is a good counter punch or a defensive blow, to use as your opponent moves towards you. (I am quoting this in its proper sequence although the result of this will not be apparent until later.)

The bed next to mine, No. 85, had been unused the whole of the time that I had been at the school, as also had No. 82, which was just around the corner in the main dormitory. When

I had arrived No. 85 had been second chief and had therefore slept on No. 2 stand (see fig. 6) until he had been drafted into the Navy just before the Christmas leave. He was a massive red-headed giant who, however, did not seem to throw his weight around, and had very little occasion to say anything to me. On the night before he left he kindly gave me a few sweets from the tuck he had brought back from 'out in town'.

Now it was No. 83's turn to go. He had reached the age when he would join a Naval Training Establishment, probably at Shotley. On the last day at school, the 'draft', consisting of all the boys of about fifteen and a half years of age, who would be leaving, would have a day 'out in town', and would bring back a variety of good things and share them around between their friends. (This was bought with their first week's Navy pay, in advance.) He arrived back just as we were turning in; he didn't seem to have much to share around, and I noticed as he made his bed up for the last time, that he did not seem very happy. Apart from the fact that he came from Plymouth I knew nothing about him.

One of the 'stations' that I would have been allocated to by this time, was the wash lavatory. It was one of the more desirable jobs in at least two respects. Firstly it was supervised by one of the junior P.O.s, and therefore the discipline usually was not very strict; in fact, with some P.O.s it was sometimes lax. Secondly, it was favoured by the smoking fraternity (the 'toggers'), for there was a boiler-room beneath with a locked iron gate which, although preventing entry, provided a nook where one could stand and smoke, blowing the fumes into the boiler-room where they were carried away through the ventilation system of the boiler. Watch was kept at strategic points, and ample warning given to enable everyone to resume their proper labours when the C.O. arrived.

There were two stands which stretched the whole length of the room (which was across the end of the main building) and there was a row of 26 basins on each side of the stands. The white enamel basins were set in slabs of slate, and there were the usual brass taps and wastes. The daily task was to clean the basins and ceramic-tiled waste trough after each time it was used and on Saturdays the floors were scrubbed with brooms and dried with squeegees and floor cloths. All the brass taps and wastes were polished. The bath, which was like a miniature swimming pool, was about three feet deep. Five or six galvanised pipes, perforated with holes, spanned it to provide a shower. Looking after the bath was a very easy job, requiring only a light scrub on Saturday, and a squeegee down after the baths each morning (Nos. 3 and 6 companies used this bath; consequently it was in use each day) (see plate 12).

It may be a good opportunity to describe a typical bath. There would be fifty-odd boys in it at one time and, although there was plenty of room in the bath itself, there wasn't quite enough room under the showers. There was therefore always a slight milling around at one end, where usually the younger ones would push in and get wet and, after getting eased out, would soap down and then try to push in to rinse off. There soon accumulated about six inches of water in the bottom, and if it came to the worst one would have to rinse oneself in this. The C.O. would control the water valves, and if things became too boisterous, or there was unwillingness to get out, the cold water would be turned on and, if this did not have the desired effect, the hot would be used which would clear the bath in record time. Leaving the bath, we would line up behind each other to parade, one at a time before the C.O. With arms stretched above the head and legs apart, one would present first the front, then after a nod from the C.O. would smartly jump about. A sharp slap on the presented bottom would indicate that all was not well, and the order to 'Get your socks off' or something similar, indicated the cause. It needed some persuasion on an icy winter's morning to leave the nice warm bath and line up in the cold.

It was some three and a half weeks after our return from leave that the first batch of 'new Jacks' arrived on a Wednesday afternoon. With three empty beds next to me I was particularly interested in who the newcomers might be, so I made my way to the bows of the ship to await their arrival. The motley batch marched in through the gateway, each clutching his few belongings, like so many refugees. They halted by the bows of the ship and, looking bewilderingly around, dispersed. I approached one or two: '7/85', I asked? 'No.' 'Belong to seven company?'

I continued. 'No', came the reply, followed by them naming their particular company. I asked several others, but I had no success.

From the first, nonchalant, obtuse, lackadaisical Rupert was not to be found. It wasn't until I was making up my bed that evening that, looking up, I saw that he had arrived. He was slightly built, rather short, bent over at the shoulders from which his ill-fitting duck suit hung about him in untidy disarray. His face was rather Oriental, with high cheek bones and slightly almond eyes. Two rather large discoloured front teeth, slightly protruding and crossed soon earned him the nickname 'Chink', a name I never called him.

He gave me that uncertain appealing look a puppy gives to a prospective new owner. My response must have been disappointing, for he slapped his belongings on his bed and gave a resigned shrug.

'What's your name?' I whispered (talking, 'spinning up', not being allowed in the dormitory). 'Rupert', he replied. 'Where do you come from?' 'Pinner', came the answer. Where on earth is Pinner, I thought?

So my next-door neighbour for the next three years had arrived. If ever a person was sent to break a C.O.'s heart it was him. He had no idea of tidiness; he would slouch along, shoulders hunched, treading on the bottoms of the backs of his trousers, oblivious to any remarks made. Of course, over the years there was an improvement, but basically he was what was called 'a bird' (scallywag).

One could never upset Rupert, he had heard it all before. If he was punished, or someone gave him a blow, it just ran off. He would give the impression that: 'this doesn't hurt me; I've suffered worse than this in the past; this is kid's stuff.' There was a shrug, or a curse, as the case may be, followed by the smile. The slight smile had a meaning all of its own. It seemed to tell all and sundry that, somehow, he still had the edge, he was on top, he would never be beaten, do what you will.

During the war (1940, I think), when things were very grim, was one of the very few occasions that I was at the pictures, and when the 'Movietone News' came on it showed the aid the

Americans were giving us in the shape of a dozen obsolete destroyers.

'And here is one of Britain's ambassadors to seal the deal', said the commentator. There was Rupert, cap on the back of his head, as large as life, complete with toothy grin, with his arms round a crowd of glamour girls. I sincerely hope he did not have to serve in one of the death traps. I have always imagined that, if he paid the supreme sacrifice, manning the gun, or whatever his duties were, at the end there would be that smile. You would never really beat Rupert.

He had one advantage, however; his home being classed as local, he was allowed, if his parents applied for permission, to go on local leave 'out of town' once every three weeks and have visitors when it was our half-day. He used to have his leave regularly, but his mother, with whom he lived, seldom visited the school.

Another new entry was No. 82. He was a tallish, slim lad with a long, lantern-jawed face, probably the longest face in the school. It did not improve matters that he had the habit, when perplexed, of dropping his jaw in a sort of yawn, and at the same time, turning his eyes sideways. He was very often perplexed. He came in for an unfair share of unpleasant jobs, and very often took the blame for some unsolved petty misdemeanour. His home was quite near the school, somewhere on the other side of Blackheath Common, and he therefore also had the advantage of local leave and visitors.

'Bouncy' was the opposite both in personality and appearance to my two former colleagues. He had the advantage of having passed the Upper Nautical entrance examination while he was at Trafalgar quarters, and at the age of about ten years he had a very promising career ahead of him. Taking No. 83's place, he actually arrived about a month after Rupert, but I am including him in the general description of my immediate neighbours. A smart eager youngster, he seemed to be enjoying his surroundings and was determined to learn and take advantage of every opportunity the school could offer. Polite, but not friendly, he had a quick smile for everyone, but did not encourage conversation. His stay in our company was short, and, before he left for No. 9, I remember him donning his new jacket with its shiny brass buttons for the first time with obvious delight. I am sure it was a prelude to a commissioned officer's uniform in later life. He was called Bouncy because of the peculiar way he used heel and toe when walking, giving him a bouncing gait.

'Inches', No. 80, was the smallest boy in the company, probably in the school. He had a round chubby face, with large brown eyes, and black hair. Strangely, he wasn't bullied though very often teased and, what may sound odd in these Spartan conditions, rather spoiled. His history, as far as could be ascertained, was of a series of children's homes, then one at Swanley in Kent which seemed to be a kind of kindergarten to our school, from where they were sent, as soon as they were old enough to look after themselves. I have often thought of 'Inches', and other boys in similar circumstances, spending the whole of their young lives in homes, and then at Greenwich School. No parents or homes to go to when leave-time arrived, they hardly knew the outside world at all, until they joined the Navy, say in 1931 or '32. A mayfly experience of life until 1939, and what then?

There were two brothers, Nos. 78 and 79, I believe. The elder, No. 78, was older and senior to me by a few months. He was a thickset boy with a strong muscular face on which he seemed to wear a perpetual leer. He was a boy with a grudge against the world, and a first-class bully ('pluck'). He went to great lengths to impress his prowess before his younger brother to the discomfort of many of the smaller boys. The younger, a small boy himself, had only recently joined the school. On one occasion (it would be during this term) we were in the dormitory during the morning work period. I had just come out of the doorway of the 'bog', when one boy came from No. 1 row on my left, and another from behind No. 79 bed on my right, and quickly held both my arms by my sides. The two brothers, at the same time, appeared and blocked my path. This all happened in the matter of seconds. The elder, pointing to my solar plexus, said 'there'. I naively looked down to see what he was pointing at, just in time to see the fist of the younger bury itself in my midriff. I fell gasping to the floor. They had picked the right time, as for some reason the rest of the boys were at the other end of the room, so no one saw the incident. For a long time afterwards, if I met No. 79 alone (the younger one) he would scuttle off. He need not have feared, for it was, and still is my philosophy, that there is enough pain caused in the world without me adding to it, so I would not be 'stirring him up' (giving him a good hiding). I had another unpleasant incident with No. 78 the next year, but more of that later.

No. 95, although not a close neighbour, was an acquaintance of mine. We would have a chat when the opportunity arose, and I would sometimes mate up with him when the company was assembled. He lived in Portsmouth, and when on leave we would very often roam around the countryside on the northern end of the town. (There were farms and open country north of Copnor in those days). He was a strange boy, a person of contradictions, not up to the top standards of neatness of the school, but not a 'scruff'. He was always seemingly indifferent to everything, yet invariably successful. He was a good scholar, always in the top classes. Although very quiet and even tempered, he packed a terrific punch. He won the runner-up medal for his weight the first year at boxing, and at least one championship afterwards. He was good at football and cricket, yet he always seemed disinterested in all these activities. In fact, even in the boxing ring he gave the impression that he was fed up with the whole thing, and just wanted to get it over and done with as soon as possible and get out. He is the only one of my 'pals' I have met since the War, and then only for a brief exchange of good wishes.

Chapter Seven

'UP HOME'

IT WAS SHORTLY after the arrival of my new neighbours that I reported to the surgery complaining of feeling unwell. What the indisposition might have been I have no idea, but suffice it to say I was 'kept up home', and sent upstairs to the 'top wards' (see plates 14 and 15).

The infirmary (see plate 37), built in 1783, as the original school, was a two-storey building of dark brick. The bottom wards had the advantage of larger windows, but otherwise both floors were identical. Reaching the top floor I was met by a nurse who ushered me into a room that did the duties of office, dispensary and surgery. (The latter in the matter of dressings and such like.) After a few preliminary questions of name, number, etc., I was led into the wards proper. These were in a large central section of the building, and as we entered I could see that although the two wards were divided by a wall, there was such a large aperture in it (it was 10ft. wide) that it could almost be described as one ward. There were about six beds and lockers on the side of each ward, the beds, unlike those at the school, being covered with blue counterpanes and were made up 'sloppy'. The floors were highly polished and there was a table in the centre of each room. I was shown my bed alongside a window that overlooked King William Walk, and I turned in.

There was always at least one duty nurse on each floor, and supervising the whole establishment was the matron. She accompanied the doctor on his morning rounds, and sometimes they would pay us a visit in the afternoon. The food was very good and plentiful, and it was a welcome change to have one's bread served already sliced and buttered (if that is the right word). The beds were made up by the nurses, and all we had to do was to take things easy and get well.

After I had been in bed for about ten days, I was surprised by the arrival of my mother. Whether my illness was serious enough, or the thought of her son being in hospital was enough to send her scurrying up to see me, I never did find out. Some six weeks were to elapse before I was discharged, and then it was as an out-patient, so it could not have been too trivial. Very serious cases, however, and operations were transferred to Seamen's Dreadnought hospital across the road. Of course, I was delighted to see my mother, who could only stay for a short time owing to the long journey; she had to travel home the same day. The most important news from her was that my aunt was paying one of her periodic visits to London in the near future, would be staying for a long time, and hoped to get accommodation near the school. This opened new avenues of thought, and from then on I could gaze out of the window and dream of going 'out in town', to say nothing of the probable frequent visits.

My main occupation during this stay was crossword puzzles. I believe that they had either just been invented or had just become popular. However, I became, and still am, a devoted fan, and would hunt through every paper and comic in my search for them. It was a welcome change to lie in bed and watch the floors being polished, not on hands and knees, but by 'dollies'. These were lead-weighted blocks of wood which were attached to broom handles by swivels. The idea was to place the block on a 'decky' (floor cloth), and push and pull it around in various directions polishing the floor. Boys were sent from each company as a 'station' to perform these and other tasks, and it was considered a very pleasant duty.

As time went on and I became accustomed to the routine I noticed that 'tonsil cases' arrived from Seamen's hospital every Thursday immediately after their operation, and on the following morning were given eggs for breakfast. Of the six or so unfortunates, there were always one or two who could not manage to eat these delicacies, and I felt it a duty not to waste such good fare. I looked forward to Thursdays, and showed a keen interest in the condition of our new arrivals each week, and in time could give a good estimate of how many eggs I would be having for breakfast next morning.

Shortly after my mother's visit, I was transferred to the other side of the ward. From the window I could see the foundations and the first courses of the new nurses' home* in what was probably the hospital grounds. It was the only place in the school where there were shrubs and grass growing. I particularly watched for the men picking up their brass tickets when they started work, and would wait for 7.30 a.m. to see if any were late, or if any tickets were left on the board. (The many men I have supervised since those days would be interested to know I made such an early start.) I remember being given cod liver oil and malt, and with a good and regular diet I was becoming fit and well again. The chaplain paid us periodic visits, and as I reached the convalescent stage he, with the matron (whom he later married) and one of the senior boys, took us out for a car ride.

Looking back, I realise that these last weeks were when things were at their lowest ebb. From then on, everything began to get better. At home, my grandfather had successfully claimed a small pension due to him for an injury received some years previously. It was only a few shillings (4s. 6d. to be precise), but as it was back-dated several months it was a welcome windfall.

My mother about this time had found work with a naval tailor owning three shops. He could sell as many collars as she could make, and as the quality of her work became known, the demand became greater. Instead of being paid ninepence each, she was now getting one shilling and threepence, and with none being returned as rejects, with the corresponding cost of the replacement tapes, this was a very substantial increase in the weekly income.

It was some time after my discharge from the infirmary during one of our assemblies in the gymnasium at midday, we were called to attention. The admiral (the 'Skipper' as he was more generally known) addressed us from the stage. It had been agreed to increase our bread ('toke') and margarine ('flop') allowance. In future it would be increased to half a loaf each instead of a third (the school loaf was smaller than its civilian

*Now Davenport House

counterpart), and we had a choice of either twice as much margarine or half as much butter as our present ration. The latter was put to a show of hands, which overwhelmingly voted for the double ration of margarine. Twice a week we had jam at tea-time, and this spread directly onto the bread without a little margarine was something I just could not stomach. To remedy this I had managed in the past to save a little each morning by eking out my breakfast portion, when we had something suitable to be eaten without it. Corned beef (as I have already described) could be melted down and the dripping used, and 'tollage' (sausage meat) could be spread on the bread direct. Now my small Bovril jar would be topped up without these sacrifices.

Chapter Eight

THE SMALL BATHING POOL

TO QUALIFY FOR one's first good conduct badge, one had to have been of good conduct both in the classroom and in one's company for nine months, and to have passed certain swimming standards. These were: to be able to swim two lengths of the bath breast-stroke, one length back-stroke; to take a dive from one side of the bath and remain submerged until reaching the opposite side; and to swim along the surface for a short distance and then 'duck dive' to pick up one of the large stones on the bottom of the pool. Each of these activities could be passed on separate occasions.

The small B.P. (bathing pool) was situated in the area at the eastern side of the school, between No. 9 classroom and the laundry. I was told to report there for instruction during my normal physical training period. It was a fairly large pool, lined with white tiles, the water being three feet six to four feet in depth, and scattered around the bottom were about four dozen large stones. Two wires were stretched along the length, about nine feet apart, and from wall to wall. They were probably used in the past as a means of training by passing a rope under the swimmer's armpits and hooking it onto a runner (pulley block) which either let him swim from one end to the other, or if there was a line attached, enabled the instructor to pull him along while he manfully kept up his breast-stroke. Around the inside of the pool, at water level, and about six inches from the side, ran a galvanised iron rail. A narrow path, about eighteen inches wide ran round three sides, and at the door end was a large space, about twelve feet wide. On the two side walls, one each side, were stowed two long wooden battens, about ten feet long with a cross-piece fastened at one end, which were used to stir the water when chloride had been added.

'Curley' Searle's duties were many and varied. He very often 'commanded' Trafalgar Quarters, stood in for any absent company officers, was to be seen 'on the gate' or doing duty at parcel's office, took regular daily seamanship classes, and was swimming 'instructor'. He was one of the characters of the school, everyone's idea of an old-time 'Jack Tar', or the owner of the rowing boat 'Saucy Sue', taking trips around the bay. He was plump, rotund, with a red face topped by his peaked cap, from under which black curls peeped. His uniform waistcoat was tightly stretched around his corpulent midriff to form an ample rest for his watch-chain, from one side pocket to the other. A formidable being was 'Curley', until you knew him. Inside he was as soft as a whipped cream walnut. When he spoke to one alone it was in a low confidential voice, but most times it was an incomprehensible rumble which sounded like a succession of Rs. This was accentuated when he was walking around puffing or roaring out orders. His orders would be first delivered in a moderate to loud voice, partly understandable, immediately followed by a loud roar when only the first syllable and on a rising and increasing note perhaps the last would be understood. Stand by your beds, would be 'Sta . . .rrrrr . . . rrreds', puff puff, and with a roar 'STR . . . RRRRRRRRREDDSS, RRR', and he would puff along.

Later, some months before I was to leave the school, I was in his seamanship class. I found him a very interesting and patient instructor. There were about six boys in the class, and he would conduct it more in the manner of a friendly chat than a lesson. I can still remember most of his teachings in spite of the fact I have had no occasion to recall them. He would drift off into personal reminiscences of the subjects which we all found very interesting. What was very important to some, but not to me personally, was that he was known never to have 'run anyone in'.

I made my unwilling way to the entrance—I had no great love of water, and was not looking forward to this new experience. I entered and reported to Curley: 'Onerstool', he puffed, which translated meant 'on the stool'. For the first three weeks of training, with the aid of a wooden stool which one stretched across, and a card on which was printed

the four movements of the breast-stroke, one went through
the motions of swimming. During this time one had a good
chance to watch the proceedings of the other boys in various
stages of training.

The first introduction to the water was made by the 'new
boys' wearing lifebelts which resembled motor inner tubes
with tapes at each end, fastened around their chests. Kneeling
as close to the edge as they could, with arms raised above
their heads, they were told to lean forward as far as possible.
At the appropriate moment Curley's foot would connect under
one of the nearest boy's shins; a quick lift, and in he would go,
and on to the next.

After the initial confusion they would make for the rail,
and in most cases, cling on for dear life. The idea was for them
to stand some three feet or so from the side, and 'swim' to the
rail, repeating the process from longer and longer distances,
until enough confidence had been gained to swim around at
will. In practice it was different however. The result was Curley
at his best. 'Awarrr . . . ail', 'AWAY . . . RRRRRAIL!! . . .
RRRRRRRRRRRAILL!!' he would boom, his voice almost
ending in a scream, the echoes ringing as his voice rose. After
he had exhausted his verbal persuasion, he would waddle over
to the edge with a 'While I'll . . .' and aim a kick at a space
about two feet above the boys' heads. His portly body would
balance precariously on the narrow ledge, hang for a moment,
and just when I expected an enormous splash, subside back
against the wall. In some obstinate cases the long stirring batten
would come into play, and with many puffs and grunts would
be brought down with a resounding thwack (always far enough
away from the boys), while his roars echoed and re-echoed. The
boys would eventually gain enough confidence and start their
training. Curley with much puffing and muttering would
waddle away to give his attention to other matters.

Although my training continued well into the next term, I
shall describe my outstanding recollections covering the whole
of the period at the swimming bath at this stage. After my
three weeks of training on the stool, it became my turn to go
through the ritual of entering the water for the first time.
After this initial shock, and regaining my breath, although I

kept as close as I could to the side I endeavoured not to touch the rail until told to do so. I soon joined the other beginners struggling to and from the rail, and by the next lesson we were all flapping our way round the pool in a clockwise direction. There was no pressure to take off one's lifebelt when one felt confident enough, one just took it off and tried to swim.

One morning we were all swimming around, when the Skipper arrived with 'Yeo'y'. I put on my best performance, and was gratified to see him point to me with his walking stick and say something to Curley. There were general nods of approval, and I had the pleasant feeling that my efforts had not been in vain. When we were drying and dressing ourselves, and our visitors had left, I noticed Curley was humming and purring away contentedly.

It was some weeks later that I decided to 'pass out' in breast-stroke and back-stroke. I had previously told Curley of my intention, and the time had come when I stood on the edge of the bath, very near to the place where a few weeks previously I had knelt, now confident that I could swim the necessary distance required. I dived, travelling as far as possible under-water to cut down the distance that I would have to swim to the end of the bath, where I turned and swam steadily until I had covered the required distance.

After a short rest I decided to try the back-stroke, which I had always found far easier than the breast-stroke. I soon completed the length of the bath without any trouble. The dive which I found even less difficult came next. Curley grunted and hummed approvingly as he marked off my name and number in the ledger.

I had now only one more task to fulfil to pass for my first badge, but for week after week I tried desperately to dive and pick up one of the stones. It seemed impossible; I just could not get down that far. At last it happened accidentally. As I was standing in the water, preparing to lean back and start swimming on my back, I felt one of the stones between my feet. As I took off, I managed to hold it between my feet, and I was surprised at how light it felt, and that I could still float by using my arms only. After several attempts I could clutch a stone between my feet and by quickly moving my knees up to my chin, I was able to grab the stone.

The next time I went to the baths I awaited a favourable opportunity when Curley's attention was drawn elsewhere, and a stone was quickly lifted and held above my head; I had passed! I might add, however, I thought Curley gave me a queer look.

The highlight of the term was the night of the boxing finals. The gym was rigged up for the occasion with the ring at the stage end, the red and green corners showing up against the white ropes and canvas, and there was plenty of bunting draped around the front of the stage. The chairs had been lined up, and we sat in our various favourite places to see the bouts. The only one I was really interested in was the welterweight final in which No. 7/95 (Bill P.) was taking part. As the various fights finished the champions were cheered by their own company and booed by the losers. Halfway through the evening, there was blind boxing. I think it was eight boxers who entered the ring and spaced themselves around the inside of the ropes, and were blindfolded. At the sound of the bell they came out swinging; and swinging is the word. Some moved slowly forward swiping mighty lefts and rights; others would move forward a pace or two and swing right round with a massive punch. When one did make contact, the victim was knocked flying. They certainly showed courage, for there was no defence, and there was no sign of hesitation; they just moved forwards slogging as they went. At the end of this performance, there were loud cheers, for there were no losers.

The welterweight contest arrived: No. 7/95 (Bill P.) was in the green corner. The bell sounded, and the combatants moved to the centre of the ring, No. 95 moving around in his unhurried manner, almost slouched around. There was a flurry of blows and the fight settled down to its three rounds. After the last round the two protagonists and the referee (one of the gymnasium instructors, 'Jimmies' as they were known) met in the centre of the ring. The judges declared the winner, the red corner, and they collected their medals, No. 95, the runner-up, taking the bronze.

As the spring term was drawing to a close, we were getting the benefit of better weather. Since I had been at the school it had been dark and cold in the mornings. There were some jobs which during this time had been extremely unpleasant, but were now quite a pleasure to perform—window-cleaning being one of them.

Two boys were detailed for this 'station' known as 'dom. windows'. First thing in the morning, after making up their beds, the two would report to the 'bog' which housed all the cleaning materials, and collected two lifelines and cleaning rags. Tying a 'bowling' around the chest at one end of the line, and a 'clove hitch' or a 'rolling hitch' round the nearest stanchion at the other, they started cleaning both the outsides and the insides. The casement windows were the easiest, as one could close one half and clean it both sides and then repeat the process with the other half, at the same time keeping the body almost in the room. Unfortunately most of them were of the sash type and one had almost to get right outside to clean them. In fact, it was far easier to get out and stand on the narrow stone ledge below the sill and do the work, bearing in mind that if your socks got wet and you marked the polished floor, it would mean polishing the deck every night for a week. But now, the sun was warm and a nice breeze from the park had a smell of grass and flowers, and one could sit on the window ledge and do a little 'scheming' (idling).

Easter leave had now arrived and, homeward again, I presented a slightly better picture than the last time. The boots now had a varnish-like polish, the results of many hours' work with the bone and brush. The almost black collar, the hallmark of the 'new Jack', was now of a pleasant medium blue. This was achieved by 'keeping them back from the laundry' and at every opportunity washing and scrubbing them to get the colour out oneself. The usual method of pressing, laying the object between mattress and lower blanket was used. Long 'fancies' and a lanyard, sent from home during the term, were worn. The cap ribbon now sported a 'tar's bow' which, with the aid of a small button in the centre and additional pieces or ribbon, cut and curled, looked more like a flower than a bow. I had also joined the amateur tailors, and now wore a neat tight jumper.

Chapter Nine

SUMMER TERM AND 'BIG B.P.'

ON THE FIRST SUNDAY after our return to the school from
Easter leave, we changed from winter to summer routine. We
discarded our thick dark navy-blue woollen jumpers, our flannel
underpants, and changed our black caps ('gibbies') for white
ones. I had bought a white cap ('white tiddley gibbie') while
on leave, so I was spared the ignominy of wearing a 'duff bag'
(white cap cover). Rupert wore his 'duff bag' with aplomb.
Any taunts or jibes were immaterial and fell like water off a
duck's back; as long as it met the requirements of the school
he was satisfied. His cap, being on the small side, had developed
a decided 'sheer' and, with the cover, had the appearance of a
German sailor's cap.

When we assembled for admiral's inspection on the Sunday
morning, it was a very much brighter-looking occasion. With
white caps, light flannel showing between the vee of our
collars instead of the dark jersey, and the sun shining, it was
a great contrast to the dullness of winter.

Just after our evening wash there was a strange bugle call,
'Into the B.P. waters, into the B.P. waters'. The large bathing
pool, or big B.P. was situated between what is now Neptune's
Hall and the park. In those days there was an area at the rear
of the gym bounded by the classrooms, toilets and B.P. (the
science room and reading room formed one side, but they
were at the southern end of the gym building), and the
entrance to the pool was from this area.

It was a very large place, sometimes holding over four
hundred boys, but usually only one or two companies went
in at a time. There was a pathway all the way round, about six
or seven feet wide, and a slatted seat fastened to the side wall
on which to put one's clothes, as the floor was soon awash.
Towels were hung on hooks around the wall.

98

This bathing pool differed, in that, instead of a deep and shallow end, the shallow area was in the middle. About thirty inches deep, it was encompassed by a railing, the middle bar of which was just above water level. Outside this rail the floor level extended about six inches, just enough to enable one to stand, providing one hung onto one of the rails. It then dropped to about four feet, well over my depth. At the door end, connecting the shallow area with the side, was a narrow bridge on the hand rails of which were fastened two high diving platforms, one on either side. There was an extra depth of water under the bridge to allow for the high diving.

The custom was for two companies to go in at any one time, starboard watches, or odd numbers, on one day, and port or even numbers the next. Thus, starboard would commence with one and three, then five and seven, leaving nine with the pool to themselves at the end. The sequence for port watch would be two and four, then six and eight. Being No. 7 company, we were unfortunate having to follow Nos. 1 and 3, as we were always left with wet towels. This could be overcome to some extent by collecting unused bathing shorts and using them, but sometimes a used towel and a rub down with one's shirt had to suffice.

The first thing was to ensure that there were sufficient drying materials. After stripping off and donning bathers, if there were any about, the 'non swimmers' would proceed over the bridge to the shallows. If they were wise they would make for the side and get outside the rails, and at least give the impression of being able to swim, before they were spotted by the 'ducking gangs'. These would collect at the rounded far end, spread out and sweep the centre for non-swimmers who, when caught, would be severely ducked. This could be a very unpleasant experience, especially as on some occasions the victim would have a wet towel wrapped around his head and therefore did not know when his head was above or below the water. On one occasion, as I was standing just outside the rails (the water was too deep elsewhere), I was seized, pushed, and bundled from one to another and finally dumped down to the bottom and stood on. The next thing I remembered was lying on the floor of the side pathway, with many faces anxiously peering down at me.

During the term, life-saving classes were available to boys interested in qualifying for a certificate, and we were all taught the basic forms of release from being held by a drowning person, and rescue. At first one would be the victim, diving into the water and threshing about; the rescuer would then approach and be clutched around the neck, waist or wrist as the case may be. He would then carry out the necessary release drill, followed by the appropriate rescue technique. The positions would then be reversed, and the victim became the rescuer. The lesson would finish with a demonstration and drill of resuscitation.

Throughout the term, during the normal swimming periods, competitions would be arranged to select the company's representatives for the aquatic sports which were held at the end of July. While these races were being run it put the ducking parties at a disadvantage because swimmers and non-swimmers alike would have to resort to the central area.

When the great day arrived the B.P. was draped with flags and bunting, and in the afternoon the spectators would arrive and crowd around the sides of the bath, and the competitions would commence: high diving, the plunge—a shallow dive, the object of which was to see who could travel the longest distance with the face submerged, the positions being chalked on the side of the bath when all forward movement ceased—the breast-stroke, relay races, which would be run off among loud cheers of encouragement, and usually a comic turn of some sort. At the end cups and shields would be awarded to the winners amid the loud cheers and boos of the spectators.

The summer term was about three weeks old when I was sent for and told that I had a visitor 'at the gate'. I was sure it was my aunt, and as I ran across the deserted parade ground (it was during school hours), I could see her standing just inside the gate, in about the same place where we had said our farewells in what seemed another age. She had been fortunate in obtaining a flat quite near to the school, and would be able to visit me regularly. I soon explained to her the procedure for applying for local leave, and with a promise that she would call on the next half day, our brief meeting ended. I returned to the classroom with my thoughts full of the change in circumstances, and my hands holding the good things my aunt had brought me, for, needless to say, she had not come empty-handed.

Periodically there was a competition to see who could win the 'cake'. The winners (there were several cakes awarded) were decided by the Skipper and 'Yeo'y', for the cleanest and neatest mess. It was judged on a Sunday morning, and after tea on the Saturday. If one's mess was taking part, all hands would stay behind to polish brasswork, spoons, knives and forks, and all the other mess utensils. The first and second cooks would have already given stools, table and floor an extra hard scrub that morning, and would endeavour to improve on this on the Sunday morning. There would probably be one or two disqualifications, cleaning the spoons with metal polish instead of whitening was the favourite, and using the block of brickdust on the woodwork when scrubbing, another. Kettles, 'bollocky cans' (pewter water jugs) and waste tins would shine like silver, and the competitors would wait breathlessly as Sam read out the winners. I was never among the lucky ones, although Jack on the next mess won it once, so at least I did get a taste.

By this time I would have been detailed for the duties of fourth cook. This, next to fifth cook, was the least-liked of the cooks' duties. After each meal, when the 'non cooks' had finally left the dining hall, at the order from Sam all the fourth cooks would rush with their heavy mess kettles down the two flights of stairs to the scullery below. There would be a jam on the small landing halfway down, and there was much pushing and shoving to get down while the water was still being served hot, and those returning with a kettle half full of boiling water struggled to get up. When at last one returned to one's mess it was to wash and wipe 17 'dips' (basins) and also to compete with the third cook with his plates, and the fifth, with his knives and forks, both of whom would be just as eager to get their particular job done. Another rather unpleasant number was second/third cook. His job was to dispose of the waste. There were two waste tins on the table, about sixteen inches by ten, and three inches deep. When competing for 'cake' these were brought up to a high stage of polish and given a prominent position in the display. After the fourth cooks had made their rush to the scullery and back, it was then the second/third's turn to take the same route, but to continue to the yard outside, which was known as the piggery. This, as one may guess, had a strong aroma which on occasions could become quite powerful, so consequently one's stay there was as short as possible. Apart from the unpleasant associations, this number was not too bad, for, with the exception of Irish stew, or spinnage, there wasn't much thrown away.

There were quite a few boys who owned roller skates, and during their free time they were to be seen gliding around the parade. From time to time Jack and I managed to borrow a pair each, and we soon became proficient skaters. One of the main activities was to start at the base of the colonnade and take advantage of the downward slope to get maximum speed, then sit on one's haunches and career amid the numerous groups walking around. This sometimes came to an abrupt end when one of the strollers would throw his jumper in front of the skates, resulting in grazed hands and knees. Another trial of skill was to speed down the parade ground and to jump the wide gully that separated the parade proper from the gravelled area. To fall short and land in the gully certainly spelt disaster.

This was the shortest term of the year, and our leisure time was fully occupied with outdoor sports and preparing for our school examinations. Each company was now running preliminary heats in various events to select its teams for the annual sports day at the end of term. As far as Jack and I were concerned, it was nice to go out into the park in the evening, but as our contribution usually ended in the first eliminators these trips were few and far between, and so we very soon lost interest in the proceedings.

When sports day arrived, we marched round to the park, wearing our number ones and white caps. (We always seemed to be fortunate with the weather; I cannot remember a dull sports day.) The area was marked off for the various events, and the running track was roped off. There were running and relay races, and long- and high-jump events were held in one corner of the arena. One or two novelty events were worth watching; the sack-race and the three-legged races had a good following; there was also the wheelbarrow race. This was held on a fairly level piece of ground on which a large rectangular frame had been erected. This was divided by wooden uprights about seven feet high, and far enough apart to wheel a barrow through. There was a contraption swinging between each pair of posts which consisted of a long wide board with a large hole in the lower end and, fixed to a small ledge on the top, was a small bucket which during the race was filled with water. The idea was that the competitors would line up some distance away, one sitting in the wheelbarrow armed with a long pole, and the driver would be standing some way off. At the signal, the drivers would race to the barrows and trundle them towards the frame, the occupants endeavouring to line up and throw their poles through the hole without tipping the pail and thereby getting doused. This was great fun and by far the most popular event.

But back to mid term. There was plenty of 'lugging up' (studying and revision) to do, as the exams. were now about to start, and I had a considerable amount of leeway to make up. My scholastic career had started at a private school, but it could not have been much good because when my parents decided to send me to an elementary school I had, in spite of my age, to start only one class from the bottom. The standards of this school were not very high. When I sat the entrance examination for Greenwich I could only do the most elementary addition, subtraction, multiplication and division. We were now doing complicated problems involving both vulgar and decimal fractions, algebra, and mensuration, all of which taxed my capabilities to the limit. In addition there were the seamanship lessons to absorb. Although there were no examinations to worry about, this subject had to be learned to the satisfaction of the instructors.

A break came when the Sunday for my local leave arrived. After divisions, which was about 10.30 a.m., before the bugle sounded the 'fall in' for church, I made my way to the gate to report. It was a strange feeling. The first time I had actually walked out of the gate of my own free will; at other times, of course, I had marched. I gave my number at the sentry box, and I was free until 7.30 that evening. As I walked along outside the railings, I realised for the first time how my outlook had changed. My world was now inside the school, and my previous life was just a dream. Outside everything seemed alien, which feeling was no doubt enhanced by the strange trams and traffic that roared by. There was a general appearance of grime, and most of the people seemed scruffy, especially the men with their untidy hair. My aunt took me up to the City and we had a very pleasant day and some very appetising food. I arrived back at the school a little sad but with an entirely different outlook from previous returns.

The examinations were now in full swing, and at this time I was also waiting to hear of the award of my first badge. In fact, I had to wait until the examinations were over and the results proclaimed before I had the gratification of receiving not only my badge, but the news that I would be joining class three, by-passing class four.

This was indeed good news as it meant that I had passed through a certain barrier. Boys who on reaching the age of 13½ and were in classes from one to three Junior, transferred to class three Senior division, and would progress to class two. Those in classes four to ten would go to classes four to six, and if and when they reached class four would have to be able to jump to class two, as class three took boys from Junior division only.

On my way to the classroom daily, I passed class three, and through the glass partition I could see a painted diagram of what I later was to learn was Pythagoras's Theorem. The white triangle, each line of which formed one side of a square, always struck me with awe, and now when I passed I had some misgivings as to whether I would be able to keep up to the new standards.

As the term came to an end, I could now review my achievements with some satisfaction. I could now swim and had some knowledge of life-saving, could skate fairly well, had a fundamental knowledge of signals, seamanship and knots, and I had done well in the classroom. Perhaps what was just as important, I now had my first 'stripe' (badge), and I had finally left the 'new Jack' stage. When going on leave this time, in addition to my 'tiddly gear' I now sported a really white flannel 'front' with a square neck (as opposed to the rounded neck of the school flannels), and a collar with hand-sewn tapes (the school tapes were all machined), both of which my mother had made for Jack and myself. (Jack was very proud of his.) When 'out in Town' I was surprised at the number of people in London who touched my collar 'for luck'. At first I was taken by surprise, and thought someone wanted to draw my attention to something, but I soon got used to it. And so I went home on my third leave—this time for six weeks.

Chapter Ten

AUTUMN TERM—CLASS THREE

IT SOON BECAME APPARENT that my new class was going to be very different from my old. I did not fail to notice that a well-worn cane rested on the master's desk ready for instant use. There was none of the tolerance that I had been accustomed to in P. D. Rice's class; everyone now sat upright in his seat and did not move, and there was certainly no attempt to talk.

Mr. Blackman was a tall middle-aged man; dark hair, a rugged face with deep-set eyes. He was a strict disciplinarian, an advocate of 'thrashing it into them', and it did not take me long to realise that I was going to be one of his main victims. Each morning, as we took our seats, we were confronted with about twenty words written on the blackboard, and given about fifteen minutes to study them. At the end of that time the blackboard was turned round and the master would dictate them to the class. We would exchange our papers with our neighbours, check them and return them with the number of errors marked. 'Those with three or more errors, stand on your seats', would snap Blackman.

'Sit down the fours. The fives. The sixes and sevens, out here in front.' There would be one cut of the cane, on the hand, for each boy. 'Eight and nines' would get the same treatment. Tens and over received one on each hand.

Now these were not easy words, the majority of which I had never heard of, and, of course, they were changed each day. Necessitated, occasional, phlegmatic were favourites, as I well remember. Taking two cuts each morning became part of the daily routine as far as I was concerned, until one particular morning, when Blackman was in a particularly bad mood. When it came my turn to receive my customary two cuts, and after I had received them, I was told to bend over, and I had an additional three on the bottom; he then followed me to my desk slashing my legs left and right. I slumped into my seat burying my head in my arms and sobbed. I stood up, and saw the looks of amazement on the faces of my colleagues, and the astounded face of Mr. Blackman as I found myself telling him that it was no use flogging me, as I just could not spell those words. I fully expected another dose of the cane, but in this case I was told to see him later. It transpired that I should have to write the mis-spelled words one hundred times. Although I had little time to spare for this form of exercise it was time well spent, for although I had the morning ritual with the cane, it wasn't so severe, and I do believe his form of punishment declined in favour of a more useful form of correction.

When Pythagoras was explained, I found the subject quite interesting, and enjoyed working on the different types of mathematical problems involved. The remainder of the work in this class was interesting, although complex. We were being prepared for the more difficult things of the Senior division.

By this time we had reverted to winter routine. I had bought a black cap while on leave, so I was now fitted up for both summer and winter as far as uniform was concerned. I welcomed the extra clothing as the cold weather was with us again, and we had the first of the pea-soup fogs that London was so famous for. It seemed to get particularly cold and damp in the Greenwich area, and during these fogs not only was vision restricted to a few feet, but it was so damp that one could imagine it was raining a fine drizzle.

I had been at the school for over a year, and had progressed up the mess table as older boys reached leaving age, or were transferred to another mess. For some unknown reason, I was at a table where there were some of the top numbers of No. 6 company, and the lower numbers of No. 7.

Our diet was again improved. This time it was an issue of a pint of milk each day, which was served instead of tea on one day and alternately for breakfast, the next morning the cocoa being made entirely of milk. I found on these mornings I could save a few sandwiches ('stungees') to be eaten during the morning break as the rather rich, greasy ship's cocoa now made with milk, was both very filling and, I might add, very tasty.

As our three-weekly period of local leave came, Jack and I (after my initial trip to the City, Jack always accompanied me on local leave) became known to the officers of the gate. 'Man' Simmonds was a short, stocky man, with clean regular features. He shared duty with 'Tug' Wilson, a tall rather red-faced man, who also did duty as 'Parcels' officer'. The parcels were served out from the bungalow opposite to the one occupied by Mr. Simmonds at the other side of the gate. When either of these were absent, 'Curley' did their duties. We would walk smartly to the sentry box, give our names and numbers, and from then on were free for the rest of the day. On our return, we would have to make sure out numbers were ticked off as we entered.

It was on one of these half-day leave periods that Jack thought of the idea. Why not go in for a 'civvy' haircut? We normally had two haircuts ('crops') each term, if we were unlucky, three. This meant that when one went on leave, at the best one hadn't enough hair for a parting, and at the worst, one was nearly bald. The usual routine was to have a 'crop' at about three or four week intervals. The idea was to get the hair cut directly we returned off leave, then programme the subsequent visits to the school barber so that about four weeks before the end of the term it was due to be cut. By visiting the civilian barber at this time and getting the back and sides trimmed, with luck a visit to the school barber would then be avoided, leaving enough hair on top for a good parting before we went on the next leave, and, in the meantime one hoped, no one would notice. We found a barber (see plate 36), who to give him credit, did not bat an eye when two almost bald boys sat down, waited their turn, and in anticipation of things to come asked for a tin of brilliantine. This scheme, with two exceptions, worked very well. The first was when almost at the end of one of the terms in which I was due for a visit to the local barber at the week-end the company officer ordered me to get a haircut. It was a disaster of the first magnitude. To disobey was unthinkable, to get a 'crop' only days before leave would mean going home with just a 'quiff' (a fringe about half an inch long left at the front), and the rest of the head almost bald. But it had to be, and as the hair fell about my shoulders, I was determined that this was not going to happen again. I will describe the second episode at a later date.

Each autumn the school was invited to a cinema in the City, and this year we were to go to the *Plaza* to see a film called 'Stella Polaris' (Pole Star). In due course a convoy of about a dozen tramcars pulled up outside the school, and as each one came abreast of the gate, there was a scramble to get on board. The smoking fraternity ('toggers') would hang back to make sure that they were on a tram that did not carry a company officer and directly we moved off out came the cigarettes.

To many, including myself, these trips were rather a mystery; we were told that we were going to a certain place, but we had no idea where it was. It was the case of boarding a tram, and not knowing how long the journey was going to last, although, of course, it was non-stop.

This was the first time I had been into a modern cinema; in fact, these places had only recently been built. The picture palaces at Portsmouth at this time were, with one exception, either converted theatres or small halls which went under such imposing names as 'Empires' or 'Regals'. The well-upholstered velvet seats, the thick plush carpets, and the rich decor was luxury beyond my imagination. The picture itself was silent, but there were sound effects during some of the scenes, such as blizzards, which impressed us all, and gave us a foretaste of the 'talkies' which were only a few months away. I arrived back at the school tired, and I was glad to get into my bed.

I had considered, from time to time, what kind of 'trade' I would like to choose when I reached the age of 13½ years. The selection of trades in the true sense of the word was small— tailors or the band. (There were also blacksmiths', painters' and carpenters' shops, but I am not sure that they remained in these trades for longer than one term before moving to another trade.) I was already quite proficient at using a sewing machine, having helped my mother by doing some of the simpler tasks such as sewing on the large tapes. In some cases when she was falling behind her schedule I would make the whole collar. I had also assisted in making some of the clothes for my brother and sister. It was also well known that 'jewing' (tailoring) was a lucrative part-time business in the Navy, and could be useful later in civilian life.

The band, however, had several advantages. Apart from the fact that I was fond of music and liked the opportunity of learning to play an instrument, there was the distinction of being the centre of attraction whenever the school was assembled for divisions, or when we were marching either inside or outside the school. Perhaps the deciding factor was that the band was very often sent out on 'engagements' to sports functions or church bazaars (we even had the honour of leading a contingent of the Royal Marines to church on one occasion), when there was usually a tea laid on for our benefit. The final temptation was that one was paid. The sum was only a modest twopence a month to start with, but it increased steadily, if slowly, to four shillings a month.

Jack and I made our way, somewhat nervously, to the band room one evening. This was situated in the semi-basement under the kitchen dining hall (see plate 32), and adjacent to the scullery. We entered a rather long, narrow room, the whole central area being occupied by two wooden music stands and long seats, one behind the other. There was sufficient room along the front to sit five boys, and the two wings could seat three on each side. The cornet players occupied the two left-hand wings and half the two centre sections, the horns the centre, baritones, euphoniums and basses, the two right wings, the drums were at the back. That is from the bandmaster's point of view. Along two sides of the room, opposite the windows, hung the instruments and at the far end in the corner was a small office, a little larger than a telephone box, which it resembled with its glass-windowed sides. The bandmaster was in this office.

Mr. Brown ('Tach' as he was known), was a short, slight, dapper little man, very smart and precise. He was the only person in the school to have a full set of whiskers, which he wore in the style of the king (George V), with a short, pointed beard. He wore his peaked cap absolutely square on his head, and his whole appearance reminded one of the period 1890–1910. He was continuously on the move, either moving his head from left to right, smoothing his moustache, or when supposed to be standing still he would be tapping the two brass buttons on his cuff with his small cane baton. A man of very few words, he held himself aloof, and he did not suffer fools or slackers lightly.

There was, in the centre of the space in front of the stands, a high stool on which he would sit and conduct. He was patient to a fault, and would have us play a few difficult bars of music over and over again until he was satisfied. Beating time with an old side drumstick, he would strike the stand in front for emphasis, and if he caught anyone not concentrating, would transfer the beat to the offender's head.

He came out of the office, and we approached and stated our desire to join the band. He gave us an appraising glance and asked us what kind of instrument we had in mind—drum, bugle, or brass—and, if the latter, which particular type would we prefer. I reviewed the long row of instruments, and decided that I did not like the blare of the bugles or cornets, and, although I rather favoured the bass, they appeared too heavy, so I settled for the euphonium. After taking the instrument down and trying to get a recognisable sound out of it, 'Tach' suggested that we might try the next size down, which is called a baritone. This seemed to suit admirably both for tone and size. Jack decided that he would also play the baritone, so, there and then, we enrolled. There were some months to go before we would be attending school, and band practice on alternate days, but in the meantime we would attend one evening each week for practice, and we were now allowed to march with the band on Sundays and on Wednesdays' march out. When the next Wednesday arrived, Jack and I proudly took our places near the rear with the buglers and, to make things look authentic, we each had a bugle hanging from our sides. As we marched along the side of Blackheath Common the bugle section struck up; it was certainly deafening. As we approached the war memorial, I noticed a group of people passing by, so I looked at Jack, he nodded, and we lifted the bugles to our lips, taking good care that we didn't make any noise. So we made our first contribution to the band.

Corporal Swift (see plate 33) ('Joey' to the school, and the band in particular) was the mainstay of the band. An ex-Greenwich boy (having been at the school from 1913-1916), he was still serving in the Royal Marines and would have been about twenty-four years of age at this time. He was perhaps a little above the average height, broad shouldered, and very upright; indeed, when playing he appeared to bend slightly backwards. Always immaculately dressed, he moved about as if he was on the parade ground. He always appeared to be in good spirits and enjoying whatever he happened to be doing. This inspired the remainder of the band, and enabled him to keep discipline without any form of punishment or bullying. There were occasions when he would engage in a little banter, especially when we were away from the school on engagements, and sometimes during the afternoons when we polished our instruments he would allow a little skylarking. Jack, in particular, after he had been in the band for some time, would engage him in these pleasantries, but they were of short duration and he would soon break off with a smile. Although he was able to play any of the instruments, he always played the cornet with the brass band, and of course led the bugle band. 'Tach' was very often in his office during the day writing and arranging the different parts, and on these occasions 'Joey' would substitute as bandmaster, beating time with his left hand and playing the cornet with his right. Unlike 'Tach', whenever we were faced with a difficult passage, he would borrow one's instrument, and give a demonstration of how it should be played.

As one might expect, Trafalgar Day, 21 October, was one of the main occasions of the year. It was celebrated on the Friday nearest to this date; it was Sunday routine in the morning, and we would be dressed in number ones. There were divisions, and if it was raining, and was therefore being held in the gym, the Skipper would give us a 'lecture' (speech). This would be followed by a short church service and then we would all march round to the local cinema to see a film. It would be something suitable for the occasion—one year it was *The Life of Nelson,* another it was *Q Ships,* which, although totally different in subject, had the same message. We always came away full of patriotism and a determination to do our duty if and when the time came.

Midday meal would be a baked dinner followed by 'foundation pong' (pudding). This was something between a Christmas pudding and a highly spiced cake, and at the table we all looked eagerly at the captain's mess as he served out the portions ('whacks'). Fortunately, there always seemed to be enough for a large portion to be served to everyone. The afternoon was a holiday, and the usual forms of activity—football and skating—could be seen on various parts of the parade ground.

At the end of the following week there was a similar commemoration—Founder's Day, 25 October; this also was held on a Friday. There were the usual divisions and march past, and as far as we were concerned a baked dinner followed by 'foundation pong', obviously named after the day it was to celebrate. It seemed rather a pity that these two events should be so close together, for we would then have to wait another year before we could partake of this favourite pudding, but one cannot alter history.

On Armistice Day, 11 November, we all went to a service in the chapel and, as one would imagine, it was quite a solemn affair. Probably all the present staff had served in the services during the War, which was only nine years earlier, and many of the boys were orphans as a result of the conflict. In the gallery were many visitors from the college and elsewhere who had lost friends and relatives. At eleven o'clock there was the two minutes' silence, followed by the 'Last Post and Reveille', played by Corporal Swift and two other Marine buglers.

This autumn term drew to a close with the assault at arms, and the fancy dress ball. My aunt attended the latter, and we had several dances together. It was to be the only time when I could put 'Yeo'y's' dancing tuition into practice, for in future I would be on the stage, playing in the band.

Chapter Eleven

A NEW YEAR. CLASS THREE, SENIOR DIVISION

SHORTLY AFTER MY RETURN from Christmas leave I had the misfortune to be included in the changes in messing arrangements that took place in the dining hall from time to time. My new mess was now on the opposite side of the hall, and I was dismayed to find that not only had I lost seniority and moved to a place nearer to the mess shelf, but I now found myself sitting next to my old enemy, No. 78, whom you may remember attacked me in the dormitory some while before.

The first few days passed without incident, but this could not last, and one dinner time it happened. Our seating places were on the far side of the table, viewed from the Square. That is to say that, when we were standing at the mess facing Sam, the table was in front of us. On this occasion when I arrived at my place, No. 78 was already standing at his, and we waited for everyone to settle before being told to sing Grace. I happened to look down, and I notice that my knife was about halfway between my plate and his fork, so I moved it back to its proper place. He immediately slid it back to its former position. I replaced it. It was snatched back and thumped alongside his fork.

'It's mine', he snarled.

'Mine', I replied, grabbing it back, and this time holding on to it, to settle ownership once and for all.

'Give it here', he shouted, to make himself heard, as we were now supposed to be singing Grace.

'Go to Hell', or words to that effect, I replied, my pent-up feelings of the past days coming to the surface. By this time we were seated and beginning our meal. 'So you think you're smart?' he continued.

'Yes', I replied, bolstered up by the knowledge that I had won that round, as I was now using the object in question.

114

'I'll see you in the gym', came the ominous retort, loud enough for all to hear. 'All right with me', I answered, now carried away with rage, and partly forced into this affirmative reply.

The words had scarcely left our lips when, like a heathfire, the news spread. 'Fight in the gym', passed from lip to lip, from mess to mess. My heart sank like a stone. Too late, I realised that I had let rage overcome prudence, and I was now in for a good hiding.

The meal finished, Grace was sung, and as we doubled out of the hall, we were both besieged by a small crowd intent on seeing that we arrived at the scene of the combat safely. As we entered the gym there was already a crowd gathered, with a space reserved for the contestants. I knew that there could be only one result of this affair, and that it would be of a short duration, for I had no previous experience of this kind of thing, and my opponent appeared to be the type that at least could dish out a hiding.

He came forward swinging a blow, but he met my fist in his face, for I had subconsciously used the left lead I had learned in my boxing lesson, and I had a longer reach. There was a roar from the crowd. We circled round eyeing each other. He came in again, and got the same treatment. This is where I missed the remainder of the training, for I had no idea how to attack, and it was apparent that I could not keep him off for ever. He moved around, bent almost double, his face scowling; he feigned and rushed, and it was all over. The next I remember was being held under the tap at the door end of the gym, and spitting blood out of my mouth.

This episode had its rewards; I was never troubled by him or anyone else for the remainder of my stay at the school, and someone in authority must have heard the details of the incident, because shortly afterwards I was transferred to another mess. There I regained my status of being halfway up the table, and stayed at this mess for the remainder of my time at the school, finally sitting in the exalted position next to the captain of the mess.

I was now at the stage when I was getting a better selection of duties as 'cook'. Third cook was my favourite. It had the advantage of being with the cooks who shared out the meals, without the disadvantage of having to scrub out the mess each morning, as numbers first and second had to. In the morning, shortly after bedmaking was finished, 'cooks to the cookhouse' would sound, and there would be a mad rush to the dining hall. In No. 7 dormitory we had the disadvantage of having to travel the whole length of the school to get to our messes. Grabbing the huge kettle one would rush to the kitchen to get the cocoa. Returning to the mess, the first job was to make sure that you had a large portion of bread and whatever else was being served out. Then, after pouring a liberal share of the cocoa for one's self (especially if it was 'milky' cocoa), and seeing that the first and second cooks were all right, also remembering the captain of the mess and, perhaps, one of your pals, the remainder was shared out more or less equally (see plate 9).

After the meal, plates had to be washed. When the fourth cook arrived with the hot water, one had to compete with him and his 'dips' (basins), and the fifth cook with his knives and forks. If it had been kippers, salmon or bacon ('fat dobs') for breakfast, obviously the fourth wanted his dips washed before the messy plates and cutlery made the water dirty, but that was his worry, and the drill was to plonk all the plates in at the first opportunity.

At dinner-time potatoes had to be collected. Selecting one of the waste tins, one would make the usual rush to the kitchen where a net full of steaming 'spuds' would be slung into one's dish. Then it was back to the mess, and after a preliminary share out, a search for the largest dinner after the other two had chosen theirs. Sometimes a little adjustment had to be made here and there before all was satisfactory. After dinner, it was washing plates again, but there were no basins to complicate things. Teatime was similar to breakfast: tea or milk to be served, and twice a week, after jam, plates had to be washed yet again.

One of the more congenial jobs in the dormitory was 'paint-work'. Two boys were employed on this job and, like 'windows', there was no direct supervision. It was usually agreed between the two which areas were to be covered and it was a good policy to keep well apart, so that you could not be accused of

22. A Greenwich boy, 1918.

23. Rear Admiral L. R. Oliphant, R.N., Retd.

24. Lieut. Commander S. T. P. Yeo, R.N., Retd.

25. Surgeon-Captain P. M. May, R.N. Retd. and Staff. Mr. Pike, extreme left, Mr. Smith extreme right.

26. March Past, Prize Day 1925.

27. Inspecting Old Boys, 1926.

28.   The Ship, taken between 1914 and 1925.

29.   View of the School from the Gymnasium.

30. The Author with his young brother and sister.

31.   At The Olympia, 1929.

32.   (*opposite above*) Band Room about 1890.

33.   (*opposite below*) At the Olympia, 1929 (detail). Corporal Swift is on the extreme right of the band, 'Tach' is on the left of the bass drum and the Author is in the front rank, on the Drum Major's left, with Jack standing next to him.

34. Part of the School buildings, now the National Maritime Museum. Note the Old Royal Observatory in the background.

35. Trafalgar Quarters.

36. Burney's Academy.

37. The Infirmary, built in 1783.

38. The Seamanship Room about 1930.

39. Returning from Church, 1932.

40. The last Boreman boy was George Frederick Berry (see page 25).

41. The last Greenwich boy was Jack Jermyn Dunn (see page 22).

42. The 'Fame' when the boys left for Holbrook, 1933.

43. The Band plays the boys out of Greenwich for the last time.

'spinning up' (talking). Providing one kept on the move and did not make the floor wet, one was normally left alone. In the winter it was rather cold work (there was no hot water), but after the initial shock it wasn't too bad, especially if one concentrated on thoroughly cleaning the two hot water pipes that ran alongside the walls.

I became troubled with a slight tenderness in the middle finger of my left hand, which developed into a swelling. I thought it might have been caused by the continual use of a broom, for at this time I had the thankless job of dining hall sweeper. I reported to the infirmary, and the doctor sent me to the sister on the first floor, called the bottom wards.

Unlike the wards above, these were light and sunny; the windows were almost twice as large as those upstairs, and here one had the feeling of being in a hospital rather than a dormitory. The next morning my finger, which had now taken on a bluish colour, had to be lanced and, after returning to my bed, I looked forward to being fit again within a few days. But this was not to be, for as this finger healed, the same thing happened to the corresponding finger of my right hand. I rather timidly drew the doctor's attention to this, and I think it came as much as a surprise to him as it did to me. In due course I had the same treatment and I waited, rather apprehensively, for further signs of tender fingers.

I wasn't really unwell, and it was rather monotonous lying in bed doing nothing. My bed was near one of the windows and I could see out into King William Walk (then known as King William Street), although I was on too low a level actually to see over the wall into the street itself. This perimeter wall formed one side of a large yard which separated the infirmary from the outside world and, joining this wall and forming the short side to this area, was a large open-sided shed. It wasn't long before I noticed there was a small door in this wall, close to the end of the shed, and this was used by some of the hospital staff as they arrived in the morning and left each evening. It was some time before I realised that the door wasn't locked. Occasionally, one of the boy orderlies would rush through this door, presumably on an errand to one of the nearby shops, and I noticed that there was no attempt at locking the door behind him. I mulled over this fact with some interest, but as my fingers grew better and I returned to duty, the whole thing was forgotten. But I was to remember it at a later date.

We were to be treated to a Shakespearean play, *The Merchant of Venice.* On the appointed day, the chairs were set out in the gym, special ones in the front row for the Skipper and other guests. Taking our places in our usual vantage points, I perched myself on one of the lower girders of the roof; we awaited developments. There was some fragile looking scenery on the stage which blended with the proscenium arch, somehow still retaining its Wedgewood blue colour with golden scroll work. There was a doorway in each of these 'wings' which was normally locked, but now the scenery separated the front from the back of the stage, these doors providing the entrance and exit.

The lights were dimmed, and only the two lamps nearest to the stage remained alight. Silence descended on the hall, there was no music, and two boys with 'lamplighter poles' dimmed the two remaining lights. The two players (husband and wife) came onto the stage, and the play began. The husband came out and took the part of Antonio, and the wife, his friend Bassanio. The story started to unfold, and we sat back and tried to make out what it was going to be about, for I doubt if anyone had even heard of Shakespeare, let alone the play in question.

After a short while, the actors left the stage. We waited patiently. After a time the situation became reminiscent of the breakdowns during the Wednesday night's pictures, and there were signs of impatience, mutterings were beginning to be heard. At last they reappeared, but this time the man was taking the part of Shylock, and the wife now in the female role of Portia. This change caused some stir in the audience and there were some earnest questions, in soft undertones on how complicated this lot was going to be, and what *would* they be up to next. However, a few sharp taps of the skipper's walking cane on the edge of the stage restored order, and the play continued. All went well for a time until the actors retired to change again, and this time to reappear as the two lovers.

After this second period of waiting some of the audience thought that this was getting a bit too much. The more vociferous and, as usual, the more knowledgeable on such matters were already giving their advice. Mutters of 'kiss her' could be heard, and others thinking of more pleasurable pursuits they could be enjoying elsewhere were not backward in giving their opinions. The Skipper called for silence and, standing in front of the stage, gave us a good dressing down, reminding us of the kindness of the two players in giving their time for our special enjoyment, and asking us to co-operate in making the evening a success. The play resumed, but now a certain flatness descended on the acting, and we all knew it would only be a matter of time before the interruptions started again.

It started with a low murmur and gradually increased to talking and then to shouting. Old friends were suddenly discovered in different parts of the room, and there were shouted enquiries as to what they thought of the performance and descriptive replies were readily given.

From my vantage point above the crowd I could only look on apprehensively and speculate on what the outcome was going to be. At last the Skipper slowly climbed the steps at the side of the stage, and there was total silence before he reached the centre. He thanked the players for their endeavours, and apologised for our behaviour. The two actors bowed and disappeared for the last time behind the scenery.

The Skipper then ordered the whole school a week of punishment, with all privileges stopped. We were in for a rough time. There was to be no local leave, no pictures or sports activities, and everyone had to move around at the double. No reading time in the evening, as lights would be dimmed directly we turned in. There would be working parties formed on Wednesday and Saturday afternoons, and those not working would be on the parade ground for drill, which in plain language meant that they would be running around all the afternoon. As I anticipated, it was a tough time.

This was to be a term of change. I was now 13½ years of age and therefore was transferred to class Three Senior division. This meant that I would only attend classes on alternate days, and would be at band practice on the remaining days of the week. I wasn't sorry to leave my old class and looked towards the Senior division with some misgivings; it was bad enough in Class Three Junior and what the more advanced subjects were going to be like, I dreaded to think. Eventually the time arrived for the transfer and we trooped into the new class-room, which logically was situated in the centre of the Senior block. I took a seat in the middle of the room, in the second row, and assessed my new master.

P. D. Snee was rather on the short side; he was dressed in a black coat and pin-stripe trousers. His black hair, well greased, was plastered straight back from the forehead, and he wore the then new-fashioned horn-rimmed spectacles. He reminded me of 'Mr. Sharp' of the Sharp's toffee advertisement. He gave us a welcoming speech in a friendly, almost genial, manner, pointing out that the examinations were to be held in July, which would determine whether we would progress to Class Two, or regress to Class Four. It was entirely in our hands which way we went, although as far as he was concerned, he was going to see that there were as few as possible going down. I viewed all this good humour with some reserve, especially when he went on: 'I have a little friend which I sometimes have to call upon, which fortunately we don't very often see; I call him my "Woolworthsey" having bought him from one of the well-known stores'. He produced a huge pencil, about nine inches long and about three quarters of an inch thick, with a metal cap and a ring fixed to one end. 'Now the form of application is this'—and he gave a demonstration of a blow to the back of the hand between the knuckles and the middle joints of the fingers—'which can be quite painful', he continued, 'so let's put him away and see that there is no occasion for him to come out.'

I must say he did not use it very often, but when he did it *was* very painful, as I found out. I had it once for inattention, and I took jolly good care that I did not have a repeat per-formance. I recollect that, in spite of this, my stay in this class was fairly happy. Mr. Snee's brisk but seemingly easy manner was subject to sudden, short, sharp storms, so it paid to keep things running as smoothly as possible. Our studies at this time became more complex, and although I cannot remember the details, I know we were involved with trigonometrical problems, and that there were many lengthy and difficult formulae to learn.

The next day was my first full day at the band-room. Jack, who was somewhat younger than myself, was still full-time at school. The instrument, which up to now I had only been allowed to borrow, became at last mine and from now on I would have the responsibility to see that it was highly polished. It had not been cleaned for months, so I had quite a job getting it to pass Corporal Swift's scrutiny. Although I could not yet take an active part, I was soon to be allowed to take my place both during the assembly each morning, when we played 'For We'd Make the Keel Row' as the boys doubled out of the gym, and the march-past on Tuesdays and Fridays, when I played the more simple bass parts. What was of great importance, I was given the gold band badge to sew onto the right sleeve of my jumper. The days were spent practising the marches to be played on the forthcoming Wednesday and Sundays and, for a change, popular tunes which 'Tach' had arranged which could be used either for dancing or for forthcoming engagements.

I still had to attend the weekly band practice, which consisted of playing the scales. In addition there was night school and seamanship classes, each one evening a week. In spite of this rate of activity, I had time to read several library books each week, devouring *Robinson Crusoe, The Swiss Family Robinson,* and all the schoolboy classics. *Poor Jack* was a great favourite of mine, and I read it several times. Each class had its library and I always had at least two books out at a time. Between turning-in and lights-out was my favourite period for reading, although if I had a particularly interesting book I would carry it around in my 'breast' (this was the space between shirt and flannel or jersey, which, with the belt around the waist, formed a large pocket. This was continually in use as there were no pockets in the duck-suits. One undid the buttons on the front of the shirt, pushed the book or other item in the space and then re-buttoned). Under these circumstances I would be a regular visitor to the square in the dining hall, for Sam would not be slow to pick me out looking at a book held under the table. I never did learn. The number of times I was caught and received my three with the brush is beyond record.

As my appetite for reading grew, so did my thirst for knowledge. I kept notebooks with facts and figures that I gleaned; the longest rivers, the highest mountains, the Seven Wonders of the World, the signs of the Zodiac, and so on. My mother had bought me a manual of seamanship (which I still have on my bookshelf), but I still made copious notes during my lessons, and derived great pleasure entering them up in my notebooks, especially colouring the flags.

Our spiritual needs were not neglected. Confirmation classes were held for boys who in the near future were to be confirmed. There was a young padre who took these classes of three or four boys at a time, where the facts of life were explained, and guidelines for Christian living taught. On 18 March, I, with about twenty others, was confirmed in the chapel by the Bishop of Woolwich, taking the Holy Sacrament for the first time. From then on I attended Holy Communion regularly at least once in three weeks. Volunteers for these services missed the whole of the Sunday morning's work; I hope I wasn't unduly influenced by this in keeping such regular attendance.

As I walked into the band-room one morning, I noticed the new drum-major being fitted with his uniform. He stood rigidly to attention, as befitted the occasion. Corporal Swift and the tailor fussed around, smoothing and tidying, pulling on the bottom of the coat and marking for alterations, checking on the length of the trousers, adjusting the sword and belt. He had the air of a superior being and looked down with rigid disdain on the rest of the band as he did on the rest of the school. He was to have a meteoric career, being promoted to second, then first-class petty officer, and by-passing and disregarding the claim of the existing second chief to chief, in record time. I do not know anything of his academic prowess, but he played cricket and football, and won medals for boxing. He belonged to my company and he was our company officer's son. Boys who were senior to him and had equal if not better claims for promotion were silent, but very bitter about this. As a chief petty officer he ruled as most men of small stature who achieve prominence rule, and although I never found him picking on anyone in particular, found it prudent to keep out of his way. Eventually he was fitted up to everyone's satisfaction, for he duly headed the band, complete with silver-headed mace.

For all the time I knew my friend Jack there were things that I did not know about him. His birthday, for instance, was never mentioned. This wasn't due to any reticence on his part, but to the practice of keeping this knowledge to oneself. Fortunately my birthday was in August, during the summer leave, but for those whose anniversary fell during the term, and was known to their colleagues, it could be a painful experience.

'Birthday bunce' was executed by a number of boys, usually three or more to each arm and leg, bouncing and dropping the unfortunate onto the floor, once for each year of his birthday. The snag was that there would be a mistake in the counting, and sometimes it ceased to be funny and, no doubt prompted a little by envy on the part of the handlers, became unpleasant. Before my time at the school, when parcels were not so plentiful as they were even then, keen eyes would watch for anyone having his number posted up notifying him that a parcel was awaiting collection, on the assumption that this signified that it was a birthday present. The unfortunate would be sought, found, and bumped.

Each year at the end of the term, the school would go to the pantomime at the *Lyceum* theatre in the Strand. The trams would arrive, and after the scramble for seats and the special requirements of the smoking fraternity were met, we would move off. This time I travelled with the band who, with their instruments, occupied one tram. We pulled up some distance from the theatre, far enough anyway to be able to form up and march into the entrance. I was allowed a place in the front rank of the band, and as it was my first appearance 'in Town' I could hardly play for excitement. Everyone eventually entered the theatre and took his seat, where there was a thorough search in the ashtrays for 'butt ends'. The band had special seating in the stalls and soon after we had settled the show commenced. We all enjoyed the performance, which included a theme song in which we all joined in led by the comedian, Jack Jackley. This must have been a good form of advertising because, on the

way back, the New Kent Road and the Old Kent Road rang
to the popular tunes as the trams wended their way towards
Greenwich.

This outing was followed shortly afterwards by the boxing
finals. There were two from my company whom I was interested in, my friend Bill, No. 7/95, who had won the runners-up
medal the previous year, and Bushnell, No. 7/2, our young
drum-major; I believe one was fighting middle-weight and one
welter-weight. Bill fought a similar contest as he did the
previous year, but this time he was more successful and had
the satisfaction of winning the gold medal. I watched the other
bout with mixed feelings. I wanted the company to have
another win, but the representative did not get my best wishes.
He put up a good show, won his contest, and received his gold
medal.

Chapter Twelve

SUMMER

THE HIGHLIGHT OF THIS SUMMER TERM was to be that a contingent of about fifty boys was going to Deauville in France for five days. It started off with a selection of 80 boys; I was included, but not Jack, and the number was gradually whittled down to 50 and two reserves. We were to give a display of the hornpipe and cutlass drill, and there were to be several boxing contests. My colleague Bill, No. 7/95, was chosen to match No. 7/2, the drum-major, to his delight, for he was considerably incensed by the latter's rapid promotion while he remained unrecognised, in spite of the fact that he was very much the senior and had a very good sports record. 'I'll kill the bleeder when I get him in the ring', he confided to me when he received the news.

On these occasions it was practice, practice and more practice. Every spare hour we had we would go through the points, cuts and thrusts of the cutlass drill, and polish up on the steps of the hornpipe, which we already knew, even when the rest of the school had gone to bed. 'Yeo'y' was in his element doing this kind of thing, and he would insist on everything being done to perfection.

At first we made do with pieces of batten for practice, but as we got nearer to the date we were issued with lifelike wooden cutlasses, with silver-painted blades and black metal hand-shields. We were formed up in five ranks in the gym one evening, and the new weapons gave us added zeal as we cut and slashed. One could imagine being with a boarding party on a wooden man-of-war about to capture a rich prize. When the opportunity presented itself, and I thought 'Yeo'y' wasn't looking, my neighbour and I put some of this teaching into practice by engaging in mortal combat. We underestimated 'Yeo'y's' eyes and ears, the result of which being that we

125

were demoted to the two reserves, and when the time finally
came we were left behind.

On their return, I asked Bill how he enjoyed the trip. He was
a boy of very few words, albeit somewhat flowery. The weather
had been fine, the food good, and the display a resounding
success. 'The fight?' I questioned. 'Gave him a bloody good
hiding', came the reply. 'He was all mashed up; they sent him
straight back to the school'. I never did find out whether this
true or not, nor do I remember seeing No. 7/2 around for a
few days, but very soon after my friend Bill was wearing a
second-class P.O.'s badge on his arm.

But to return to the beginning of the term. I was given
permission to wear my second good conduct stripe, which one
was entitled to six months after the first. I was now beginning
to consider myself an 'old Jack', although I would have to wait
another six months and get another badge before I really
qualified as such. Being in the band, the only time I now
mustered with my company was for meals, going to the wash
lavatory, and for bed, and I therefore missed all the drilling
and discipline at morning divisions, march-past and Sunday
inspection. In fact, when I was doing the duties of cooks that
prepared meals, I only mustered twice a day, for wash and bed.
Like the now defunct old-time 'stripey' in the Navy (these were
men who spent their whole career in the Navy without gaining
any promotion, satisfied in leaving as they joined, excepting
three good-conduct badges), I now knew the ropes: to be able
to obey orders without the desperate rush of early times, yet
not far enough back to be caught in the last three or six, to
be just out of view when someone was required for some
unpleasant task, and knowing how far to go with some of the
P.O.s without qualifying for punishment.

It was about this time when I was incidental in improving
our Spartan living. I was included in a batch of about a dozen
boys chosen to attend a garden party given by the good ladies
of Greenwich. It was held in the garden of one of the large
houses on the borders of Blackheath—possibly the Convent
school in Chesterfield Walk. It was very upper class, with
expensive garden-party dresses and wide-brimmed, Ascot-type
hats. We were liberally fed with cakes and lemonade, and

there was a Wall's ice-cream tricycle in attendance, from which we were allowed one free ice-cream. I must have shown my delight as I was consuming my portion, because one of the good ladies enquired when I had last had the pleasure of eating ice-cream. I naively thought she meant this new pre-packed product that we were now eating, which tasted entirely different to that of the Italian 'Joey's' at home, who served their halfpenny cornets from a richly-painted barrow decorated with pictures of Italy.

'I have never had the pleasure of eating it at all', I replied. 'It's the first time I've tasted it.' The good soul was so flabbergasted at this, that, calling over her immediate neighbours as witnesses, she again asked the question and again I gave the same reply. This sent them off in a flurry and, after questioning some of the other boys who had either overheard the conversation and had hopes of further supplies by giving the same answer or had in fact never been in the position to enjoy this delicacy, caused them to break out into exclamations of concern.

It was some few weeks later, when I had forgotten all about this incident, that, on the parade early one Saturday afternoon, my attention was drawn towards a crowd which had collected under the trees near the parcels' office. I thought there might be a fight or something else of interest, so I hurried over. There were about seventy or eighty boys all bunched up in a tight circle facing inwards, each with one arm upstretched. When I got closer I could see that in the centre, among the forest of arms, was a scraggy figure trying to serve bars of ice-cream from his box tricycle. The fact that he was seated on his machine gave him additional height but, so tightly was he hemmed in, it was almost impossible for him to serve. It was fortunate that his goods were inside the box, and that the access hole was only large enough for him to get one arm into the box to serve, otherwise his goods would have vanished before his eyes. In a very short while he had sold out, and made several unsuccessful attempts to dismount and go to the 'phone to request replenishments. At last he managed to convince them that he did not have an inexhaustible supply and that further stocks would arrive only if he were allowed to get a message to his firm, and he was allowed to leave his machine and make his way to the sentry box at the gate. He was a pathetic figure, his peaked cap pushed to one side, a rough butcher's apron round a thin waist, cycle-clipped trousers accentuating his skinny legs, ending in a pair of down-at-heel shoes. My heart sank for the poor devil, as I knew that these types of salesmen worked on commission, and in those days, many miles would have to be travelled in all weathers to make even a modest living. At least he was onto a good thing while he was allowed into the school, which from then on became a regular attraction during our half days off work. Needless to say he did not get rich on my custom, for all I could afford was a 'Snowfruit' at very infrequent intervals.

All the tradesmen's activities were carried out in various 'shops' in the area between No. 6 dormitory and the eastern boundary wall (see fig. 8). This was called the back yard. There was a long wooden building which housed the tailors at one end; next door was the linen repair shop, the carpenter's, which was the largest, next, and the painter's at the other end. It was seldom necessary for us to visit any of these establishments, but there was the odd occasion. We did our own minor repairs, and major repairs were seldom necessary to our blue suits or duck suits. Linen was examined each week when it went to the laundry, and any item needing repair was passed onto the appropriate 'shop'.

Permission could be obtained from the master tailor to 'have a look in the bin' for discarded blue suits, the materials of which could be used for fancy dress, or any other hobby one might have at the time. 'Housewives', which consisted of a piece of material about twelve inches long and about five inches wide with a pocket formed in one end, the remainder lined with silk, were fitted out to the owner's own design to take needles, darning wool, reels of cotton and so on. They were rolled up and secured with a length of fancy tape when not required, and nearly every boy had one.

Jack and I decided that we would try to get a pair of discarded trousers, preferably from someone who had just left for the Navy, and alter them to make a pair of 'Tar's' trousers. It was considered smart to have the widest trouser bottoms possible, and as this was usually determined by the

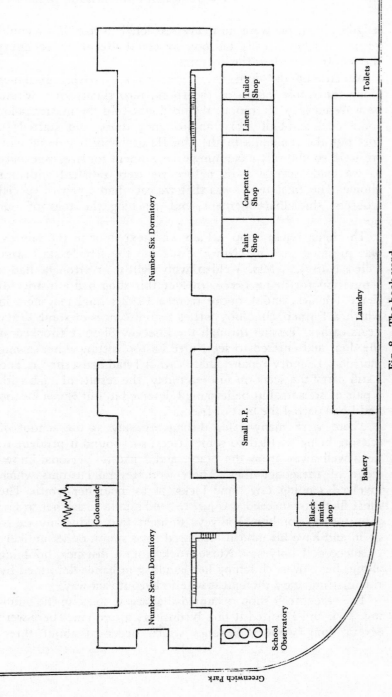

Fig. 8. The back yard.

length of leg, we were normally restricted to size. If we could get a pair from a really tall boy we could alter them, retaining the required width at the bottoms.

We entered the door; there were rows of sewing machines along the whole length of the room, now silent, for it would be a Wednesday afternoon. We no doubt told the master tailor some cock-and-bull story about fancy dress, and started to sort out the remnants in the bin. He probably wondered why we were so choosily examining each garment for size, especially as we made several visits before we were satisfied with our choice. The final result was that we each had a pair of special trousers, threadbare perhaps, but reaching the toes of our boots.

The linen repair shop, which was next door to the tailor's, was presided over by 'Nurse' Tock (all the female staff were called Nurse), a Mrs. Welden who rightly or wrongly had a reputation for being fierce. In fact this shop had a history of fierce females, and I quote from a 1932 school magazine in which a former schoolboy writes reminiscences of some thirty years earlier. 'Passing through the Checkey Shop, I knocked at the door and entered to see Nurse Eastop, sitting at her sewing machine. Laundry repairs, that is what I had had a shot at, and I still carry the scars on my leg today, the results of a jab with a pair of scissors, but believe me I deserved it, but Nurse Eastop and I had parted the best of friends'.

There were many tales during my stay at the school of scissors being wielded to some effect, so I found it prudent to keep well away from the place, and I had no personal knowledge of these activities. There were several customs which involved sending raw 'new Jacks' in to incur her wrath. The most likely to succeed was just to send him in to ask her to sew a button on for him. I always thought that asking anyone to go in and have his mouth measured for a spoon rather unlikely to succeed. I only saw Nurse Tock from a distance, hobbling along, bent over, clutching her handbag in hands deformed by rheumatism, and I thought it wise to keep it that way.

The carpenter's shop occupied the largest space in the building. Jack and I visited it one Wednesday afternoon. There were several long wooden benches which occupied about three-quarters of the area, where locker drawers, stools, desks and other items were in the process of being repaired, and we watched with some admiration the 'chippies' at work. The remaining space was occupied by a contraption which consisted of a large wheel, about seven feet in diameter, with a handle on each side for turning (see fig. 9). There was a deep groove cut in the outer edge to take a rather thick rope which drove a circular saw or lathe on a small bench about twenty feet away. We hung around and watched the carpenters at work; the boys who usually worked there were, of course, having the half day off like ourselves. We were soon invited to man the machine, and were delighted to be able to help. We spent a strenuous afternoon, but this did not deter us from making this one of our main Wednesday afternoon pastimes. After a while, I persuaded one of the men to give me a piece of soft pine, and I carved myself a model of a sailing ship. I kept it in my locker drawer for weeks, until just before leave I hastily opened the drawer, and my ship was dismasted. We gradually became tired of the carpenter's shop, but I never lost my interest in woodworking.

The paint shop was the last in this building, and I had no occasion to visit it. There was one afternoon, however, when we decided to carve our numbers and the date on the paint shop window frame. Instead of the proper date we decided to carve 1934, some six years ahead. As I carved I tried to imagine this date, which to me seemed to be in another century, for I could only remember the 1920s, and I was not to know that by that date the school itself would have moved.

The laundry was opposite these shops, and I have previously described the interior. Apart from the small B.P. the two remaining places of interest in use at this time were the bakery and the blacksmiths. The former was only interesting if you could catch one of the baker boys when leaving with his daily loaf (still warm) and from whom one could buy a loaf for twopence. The blacksmiths next door I visited several times, chiefly to replace wheels that had come off skates, but it did not have the attraction of the carpenters.

From the very beginning of the school, navigation has been on the curriculum. To achieve the high standard to which it has been associated over the years, it is not surprising that when

the school was built at Greenwich it had its own observatory. Situated in the south-eastern corner adjacent to the Upper Nautical classrooms, it was built in 1840. It had the appearance of a large private house with its own shingle-covered yard at the back. This yard was separated from the area which housed the various 'shops' by a wall in which was a small doorway, through which we struggled to push on our way from the dormitory fire-escape to the wash lavatory each morning. The building itself was of Portland stone, matching the design of the rest of the school. Originally there were two revolving wooden observation domes on the roof, each with sliding shutters fitted to enable observations to be made. In 1863 it is described as 'a two storey building which contains Quadrants, Sextants, Theodolites, Transit Circles, large and small Telescopes, Binoculars, etc . . .'. At a later date, an extension was added, with an additional dome. Each of these domes could be synchronised to a star so that it followed its movements through the heavens, and observations could be made at any time without resetting the telescope (see plate 6).

A story is told that in the late 1800s a class was selected to go to the observatory after the remainder had gone to bed. One of the boys, looking for a certain star, appeared to be rather a long time finding it, and at last the nautical master became impatient and asked, 'Now then, Jones, haven't you found that star yet?' 'No sir', came the reply. 'Get out of my way boy', said the master, going to the instrument. 'Let me see.' The master put his eye to the telescope only to find that the shutters of the revolving tower hadn't been opened. It was difficult to live down a 'howler' like that, as one may well imagine. The joke stuck, and from then on he was known as 'Jones, who observed Formalhault through the shutters'.

One of the many navigators who learned their craft at the school and who was taught his skill in this observatory was a Captain Pimm. He was a Boreman boy, and on leaving the school in the 1890s went with his friend, who had left at the same time, to the Royal Albert Docks to see if they could get taken on as apprentices on one of the ships. They were still dressed in their uniforms, and they approached a sailing ship which appealed to them as a good prospect, boarded, and asked to see the captain. They were directed to his cabin and explained that they had just passed out of the Royal Hospital Upper Nautical School, and wanted to go to sea as apprentices; they had been schooled in navigation, seamanship, and nautical astronomy. Pimm also stated that he had won a silver medal for navigation and the use of the sextant.

The captain was both interested and impressed, and said, 'Well, I cannot take you both, but I think the owners would agree to take one'. It was arranged for them to see the owners who, as the captain had stated, would only agree to take one apprentice. Pimm was selected, and so the friends had to part company. Shortly after, the ship finished loading and they set sail for New York.

From the time the pilot left, Pimm took sights of the sun and stars, to ascertain latitude and longitude, which he reported to the captain throughout the voyage. On arrival the captain was so impressed that he asked Pimm to go ashore with him to the 'Captain's Room', which in most ports is a sort of captain's club, where they can meet and discuss matters of common interest. At the time there were several captains present, and Pimm was duly presented to them. His captain stated that, 'This apprentice boy of mine has navigated my ship all the way from the English Channel, accurately and with confidence, to this harbour; I do not think it has ever been done before and he should be congratulated on his efforts. I am sure he will become a very skilled navigator'.

By 1926 the observatory had fallen into disuse. It was a favourite place for climbing over the wall and getting caught. The Upper Nautical classes (which included the Boremans) still made their sextant readings just outside their classrooms, adjacent to the old building, and no doubt produced some navigators just as skilled as Captain Pimm.

Second cook was another desirable duty. At breakfast and teatime he had to collect loaves from the bread store which was attached to the kitchen. Midday it was beans, cabbage or peas. On Mondays, Tuesdays and Fridays, when it was corned beef, Irish stew and fish, there was nothing for him to do, except fill the 'bollicky can' with water which he had to do daily. In the morning, with the first cook, he had to scrub out the mess but after the midday meal and at teatime there was again nothing for him to do. When mess gear had to be polished he had to bring the two pewter jugs up to a silver-like finish.

First cook collected the margarine ('flop') at breakfast and at teatime, and twice a week instead of margarine there was jam. At dinner-time the meat ('fat wang') had to be collected. He had to wash the spoons when they were used and to polish them once a week. With the second cook he scrubbed out in the morning. This involved scrubbing the table, stools and floor. Saturday was by far the worst morning, for instead of taking the normal hour to do the work it had to be spread over four hours.

Directly the boys left the dining-room, the mess would be swept and all the mess gear normally kept on the table removed onto the mess shelf, while the third, fourth and fifth cooks were performing their tasks. When they had completed and left, Sam would call for silence by having the bugler sound the 'G'; he would then give the order to get the hot water. There was a rush to the scullery with the mess buckets to get there first. While this was going on two large drums, one at each end of the dining-hall, would be trundled into place and filled with boiling water and soft soap.

A start would be made scrubbing the tables, and the boys normally employed as sweepers would now go around bailing out the soft soap onto the tables, while the cooks scrubbed furiously. This would last for some time. Sam, suitably clad in seaboots, would be walking up and down the gangway to see that there was no slacking. After about half an hour on the tables, which would be rinsed and thoroughly dried, a start would be made on the stools, not only the tops, but the undersides and the legs. By this time the floor was awash with foaming, soapy water. The stools were thoroughly dried, especially the bottoms of the legs, and lifted onto the table. Then, at the end of the morning, they were put back onto the floor. This on a Saturday was really an ordeal, for we spent what seemed to be an endless time on each patch, and the ever-watchful eye of Sam saw that there was no slowing down.

At long last, we would mop up the central passageway and all would be finished.

The sun would shine through the windows on to the now gleaming white woodwork, and one would carefully tiptoe across the wet floor to the mess shelf and retrieve a carefully hidden 'stungee' from behind the plates. It really tasted good.

The canteen was in the left-hand corner of the gymnasium, and there was a small pigeon-hole type of serving hatch where we made our purchases. Stamps were taken as well as postal orders, and with a three-halfpenny stamp one could buy a sizeable bag of liquorice allsorts, chocolate caramels, or a large slice of cake.

There was always a queue lined up along the wall waiting to be served, especially on Saturdays, and this led to several types of unfair practice by those who were not prepared to wait.

———————

During the term the band went to quite a few engagements and, as a regular member, I was always included. There was one at a girls' school near Croydon on a Saturday afternoon. We all looked forward to this as our interest did not finish with the prospect of a good tea—we were eager to see what the girls were like. The time arrived and we boarded the tram. We seemed to be travelling for a considerable time, changed trams several times and I believe we were mis-directed at one stage, for when we finally arrived at our destination it was only to find that we were too late, and the sports had finished. As we viewed the refreshment tent, with its used cups and saucers spread over the stained table-cloths, our jaws dropped; it appeared that we had missed both the girls, and what was far more important, our tea.

The situation was saved when one of the principals arrived. She conducted us to a smaller tent where we were to behold two tables laid out with piles of cakes and sandwiches, which we proceeded to demolish in record time. We finished our meal, and with lighter hearts and heavier stomachs, departed homewards. When we reached the place where we had to change trams for some reason or other we had to run for it.

It must have been an unusual sight to see several dozen sailor boys with their instruments under their arms running for the tram, especially as they left behind a trail of cakes which were being shaken out of the bags our instruments were wrapped in.

We went to see the Royal Tournament at Olympia during each summer term. This involved rather a long march from the school to New Cross Gate station, the nearest for the Metropolitan line. The first thing on arrival at the station was a rush to the cigarette machines. Not only the smokers, but anyone who had the money to spare, would buy them for there was a lucrative exchange rate back at the school. A packet of five cost twopence, and one could sell them for at least twopence each.

My first visit (the previous year) was also my first experience of travelling in an underground train and I did not enjoy it very much. It was a special train, hired exclusively for us for the trip, and therefore did not stop at any station. After the first few hundred yards, the train entered the underground tunnel and there was nothing to see except the odd station as we flashed by, and I was soon wondering how long this monotonous journey was going to last. I was in a carriage where there was no officer in charge, so it wasn't long before the 'toggers' were in full blast, and in all it was a miserable time. This year I was with the band and Corporal Swift was with us, so there was some discipline maintained. It was a good show, and we had the opportunity of showing what we could do when we proudly marched into, and out of, the stadium.

During the term I had enjoyed a great deal of swimming, and I was by now too old a hand to be caught by the ducking gangs, and was also a fast enough swimmer to be able to get out of their way. At the start of the term, I had occasionally 'oxed' with No. 6 company, and Jack would come in with No. 7 the following night. When we found that we were unobserved we made it a regular practice and therefore 'had a dip' every night. In the end I believe hardly anyone knew which company either of us was in. In addition we were sometimes allowed in the swimming pool during our afternoon's band practice if it was a very hot day. On our now regular days of local leave the first place we visited was the newly-built local swimming baths.

The examinations were laboriously sweated out in the hot July heat; fortunately, we were now only at classes every other day, which made things less fatiguing. The eagerly-awaited results, when they came, brought the good news that I would be going to Class Two at the beginning of next term.

The past months in Class Three had passed uneventfully, although I had been one of the few to feel the weight of 'Woolworthsey'. It was a hot summer afternoon, and the sun shone through the window on to my blue serge uniform and I could hardly keep my eyes open. I expect the rest of the class was in the same lethargic mood because P.D. Snee was showing signs of impatience as he was going into detail on some particular subject. Suddenly he stopped, and pointing an irate finger at me, asked me to repeat his last sentence. I must have been dozing, for I had no more idea than the man in the moon of what he had been talking about.

'Come out here', he ordered. Immediately all the class was now wide awake. 'Get Woolworthsey off my desk and bring it to me', he continued. I unwillingly obeyed, handing him the large pencil. Holding my left arm firmly under his, he snapped, 'Limp, limp, hold your hand limp', and to emphasise his meaning he tapped the ends of my fingers with the stick. Then suddenly I felt as if my fingers had been chopped off. When the life started to come back into my hand, the pain was far worse than any caning that I had ever received, and it was certainly a good cure for inattention.

Prize-giving day was always held on a Friday, and it was routine as for Sunday. Our white caps would have been specially blanco'd on the previous day, extra attention being paid to our uniforms and our boots, as we would soon be inspected by some dignitary who later would be giving out the prizes. The bugler would sound the 'fall in', and the whole school would assemble on the parade ground for divisions. The band would then march round to our position on the port side of the ship, facing the columns. My regular place in the band was in the front row, just to the left of the drum-major.

We would start to play one of our best-known numbers, 'Over the Waves' ('The Skater's Waltz'), or 'Waters of the

Danube', the procession of officers would leave the Queen's House, and the inspection would commence. Relatives and friends who had arrived to see the prize-giving were watching from the perimeter, and there would be a crowd outside looking through the railings. All the boys were at their best and eager to put on a good show.

At the front of the columns was a contingent of the newly-formed Old Boys' Association, their civilian clothes, trilby hats and occasional walking-sticks contrasting with the rest of the parade. This Association, inaugurated in September 1925, three years before, by the then Captain Oliphant, rapidly expanded. The first branch was formed at Chatham, closely followed by one at London and one at Portsmouth, and the members attended the first annual reunion on Prize Day 1926 (see plate 27). By 1927 the membership exceeded one thousand, and regular monthly meetings, whist drives, dances and other social activities were arranged, including an annual visit to the school on prize day.

The march-past (see plate 26) went with a swing, the Old Boys acquitting themselves favourably before their more elderly colleagues. At the end of the ceremony we were dismissed to enjoy a well-earned dinner.

In the afternoon the chairs were brought out into the gymnasium and the prizes were awarded. Jack and I, not being very interested in this part of the proceedings, slipped away at the first opportunity and took a walk up and down our favourite part of the parade under the trees.

After the prize-giving there was a diversion when some of the Old Boys tossed coins for the boys to scramble for. It was all good fun while it lasted, but there wasn't much money to throw around in those days, so this form of amusement was short-lived. They were eager to contact the present holders of their numbers ('tallies'), and now and again there was a shout of 'Anyone seen 3/50?' or whatever the number might be. Sometimes he would be found, and there were usually a few coins passed to the lucky one. There were some old members of over eighty years of age, and they must have been in the Service when steam was first used in warships as a means of propulsion, and certainly on the first ironclads. The bugle sounded for supper, and it was the signal for all the guests to depart to their homes, and for us to change into our duck suits and continue our usual routine.

Cadders Eve came round again, and the blacking tins had been emptied by those who wanted to even up an old score, or those who thought it a good opportunity to do a little rough stuff. It was a nice sunny summer evening and Jack and I spent our time walking up and down just inside the railings. We very often passed a quiet evening, winter or summer, walking (quarter-deck fashion) this part of the ground, which being covered with shingle was shunned by the boys playing games. It was getting near supper time, and we entered the doorway of the gym. I was talking and looking Jack straight in the face, when suddenly I was horrified to see a large blacking brush strike him right between the eyes. He collapsed at my feet, and as I bent over him, a swelling the size of a hen's egg slowly formed on his forehead. I nearly died with fright, thinking that he had been killed. A crowd soon gathered and he was carried unceremoniously, shoulder high, to the infirmary. I left him as they entered the surgery, and from then on had no way of contacting him to find out how badly he was hurt. As the few remaining days of the term passed I began to wonder if he would be fit enough to go on leave with the rest of us on the Wednesday. He did, in fact, remain in the hospital until the latter end of the following week, and therefore returned from leave a week later than the rest of us. It was some eight weeks later that I saw him again. Of course, he remembered nothing of the incident, but he enjoyed the experience of going on leave on his own and, better still, being on leave when the remainder of us had returned and were working.

Chapter Thirteen

AUTUMN TERM. CLASS TWO,
SENIOR DIVISION

I SELECTED ONE OF THE FRONT ROW desks when I entered my new classroom. It was second in from the blackboard, and there were four desks on my left to complete the front row. After I had put my books and belongings in the desk I had time to view my new surroundings. Unlike my previous classrooms which, with the exception of a map or two, had just bare, painted walls, this one had three of the walls decorated with rows of picture postcards. In front of the class, behind the desk and blackboards, were several glass cabinets, and I was busily engaged trying to see what they contained when the master entered.

P.D. Woods came into the room and stood in front of the class, just in front of my desk. Very smart and upright, wearing a tweed suit and highly polished brown shoes, he had all the characteristics of a soldier. A neatly-clipped 'military' moustache and a tanned face that told of many years in hot foreign parts emphasised my theory. When he spoke, it was in a smart, crisp manner, and I speculated that he had been an army officer, or perhaps an army schoolmaster.

He went over to the cupboard and took out the cane, and waved it around for all to see. My heart sank. I fervently hoped we were not going to have 12 months of this kind of teaching, with the cane as a regular part of the curriculum.

'Well, boys, it is my custom to let everyone see the cane at the first opportunity', he said, moving over to the cupboard and putting it away, 'and to show you all where it is kept. It is my intention to let it stay there until this time next term, and I might say it very, very seldom has to be used (my spirits rose at this news), but if I do have to bring it out', he said, jutting out his chin, 'the culprit will be for it'. He was as good as his word; I don't remember him ever using the cane all the time I was in his class. He had a very good cure for anyone trying to take advantage. The offender would be told to stand in front of the class where he would be subjected to P.D. Woods' satire, which would be carried out as he was teaching, usually while he was writing on the blackboard, until the victim was thoroughly embarrassed, and sometimes brought to tears. 'You may have noticed', he continued, 'the postcards on the walls and the objects in the glass cases; they are there for your benefit. Any time, during the morning or afternoon breaks, if it is raining for instance, you may look around, and when the opportunity arises, ask questions'.

We got down to our lessons, and two things became quickly apparent. One was that he preferred to teach from the black-board, and would invariably start a lesson by writing something on the blackboard. Secondly, after the first few days, he seemed to know the home town of most of the boys in his class. It would be when he was writing some lengthy problem on the blackboard that was the occasion for someone to do a little talking while the master's back was turned towards the class. 'Because Hull City lost four goals to one on Saturday, there is no need for anyone to go into the details about the match with his neighbour', 'Woody' would say over his shoulder. Everyone would look around to see who this was meant for, and there would be whispers of 'shut up' to the culprit from the remainder of the class, for no one wanted to upset the master.

There was one particular lad, who had been in the class for some time, who was a particular target for P.D. Woods' good humoured wit. He came from Ireland, and he was a small boy with a pale face accentuated by a pair of large dark eyes and black hair. I always imagined him as an orphan, one of the lonely boys who had lived in one orphanage after another, and was now in his last home before joining one of the Services. His name was McIlroy and the master pronounced it as one syllable with just a slight emphasis on the Mc. He was a bit of an imp, on the quiet, and a perfect foil for P.D. Woods' wit. He sat in the front row, on my extreme left, ideally situated for the master to talk to and also to keep his eye on. McIlroy, knowing he was slightly favoured, would go as far as he dare and the result made a very happy atmosphere in the class,

although 'Woody' was a strict disciplinarian, and these pleasantries, although frequent, were of short duration. We would often
start a lesson with the master going to the blackboard and
saying, 'Now if McIlroy is ready', or 'If Mr. McIlroy will allow
us to proceed.' The boy would beam, and wriggle about in
his seat, and everyone would be in a good mood to start the
lesson.

The evening that I had to attend evening class, I duly took
my seat and waited for the lesson to start. All the boys were
soon seated in their places, and 'Woody' came in and stood in
front of the class. 'Now, boys', he started, 'we have a certain
amount of work to do this evening, and the quicker we can
finish it the sooner we can get down to something more interesting. We have five arithmetical problems to solve, and we will
go through them stage by stage, one by one round the class,
starting with our friend from Chatham on the right here.' The
first boy started off, 'Woody' writing the calculations on the
board as the boy gave him the instructions. 'Next', would call
'Woody', and the second boy would carry on. No one was
allowed to give any assistance, but when it became apparent
that a boy could not carry on, there would be a sharp 'Next'
from the master, and progress would be maintained. To keep
us all on our toes, he would from time to time break the
sequence and continue from a different part of the room.
'The boy from Portsmouth in the third row, carry on', he
would suddenly bark, and so it would go on. It was remarkable
how quickly we finished our task, and when we did so, I sat
back and awaited the next move.

'I hope you boys have been looking at the photographs and
items of interest around the room. Now has anyone any
questions he would like to ask?'

About half the boys in the class put their hands up, and one
was selected to put his question. We settled down as 'Woody'
soon warmed to his subject about plants, peoples and customs
of faraway lands. India and Rhodesia were his favourite
subjects, and I assumed that he had served many years in these
places. We listened with rapt attention as he told us of the
strange customs of the Parsees in India; how they placed their
dead on gratings at the top of specially built towers called

Towers of Silence for the vultures to eat the flesh off the bones, which were subsequently given a ritual burial.

He told of the sacred river Ganges, where the Hindus sometimes travelled hundreds of miles to bathe in its waters and to carry out special rites, one of which was to fasten a candle to a small improvised raft, light it, and float it down the river. If it remained alight until it disappeared from sight, it was considered that good fortune was in store and one's wishes would be fulfilled.

Another evening it would be Rhodesia, and it was clear that Cecil Rhodes was one of 'Woody's' ideal men, and the land that he did so much to discover and develop was near to his heart.

During the first week in my new class it was the Monday, Wednesday and Friday only that I attended, and therefore it was not until the second week that I was at class on a Thursday. When I entered the room the first thing I noticed was a tin of pineapple chunks standing in a prominent position on the master's desk. We had just settled in our seats, and I was beginning to wonder what the significance of the tin of fruit was, when my thoughts were interrupted. 'Attention, boys', said 'Woody', in his rather sharp clipped manner. 'Every Thursday we have a test, and the boy with the highest marks wins the pineapple chunks', and, turning to the blackboard, 'Here are the questions'.

We toiled all day, my hopes of winning the prize diminishing as the day wore on; we had time, however, for one of 'Woody's' talks before we finished the day. This was by far the best class I had been in, the standard was very high and I found it very difficult to keep up with the remainder of the class. This wasn't surprising as in only twenty months or so I had reached a quite high standard of education compared with the almost illiterate state in which I had entered the school. With my musical parts becoming more complex and seamanship to be absorbed, I was beginning to suffer from a kind of mental indigestion. On the Monday the lucky winner was called out to the front to receive his prize. We all looked on with envious eyes, for preserved fruits were only seen on birthdays and at Christmas.

On one occasion we were coming to the end of our midday meal, when I noticed that there was a slight commotion on the 'square'. Sam had started to walk towards our end of the hall and he seemed to be making enquiries. He first went to one side of the gangway and, seemingly not satisfied, came over to our side, shouting to make himself heard over the babble of voices and the rattle of cutlery. Faster than Sam, the word went from mess to mess until it reached us: 'Anyone in the band?' 'I am', I shouted, standing up without any thought of the reason for the enquiry. 'On the Square', shouted Sam, nodding towards the centre of the hall. I promptly obeyed, only too happy to be making the familiar trek without the usual painful sequel. 'Duty bugler', snapped Sam as he made his way to the mess stool he usually stood on.

I walked over to the small table and picked up the bugle. It seemed useless to try to tell Sam that I had never blown a note on a bugle in my life. In any case, he was now standing on his perch, looking around, preparing to give the orders to finish the meal, and I could not even contemplate interrupting the normal course of events which went like clockwork from day to day. Putting the red plaited cord over my shoulder, I let the instrument hang down against my thigh, placed my right hand on the bugle, and stood to attention. I might as well look the part if nothing else. The mouthpiece was only half the size of that on my instrument and I was doubtful if I would be able to make any recognisable noise emerge when the time came. Pushing my fist into the bell to muffle the noise I tried a few tentative notes, but a disapproving look from Sam cut short that form of practice. 'G', shouted Sam hoarsely, nodding towards me. Lifting the bugle up slowly, in a most professional manner, I blew a long note. To my surprise it sounded like 'G' and, in my nervous state, I made it sound so loud that the reaction was immediate and there was complete silence. The next call, after Sam had finished what he had to say and the boys had sung Grace, would be the 'carry on'. If we consider 'G' as doh, the 'carry on' was two notes, doh-me, and I knew what the result would be if I cracked a note— derisive cheers and catcalls. The thought of having to sound the 'still', which would be used if things got too noisy and one wanted silence immediately, left me cold, for one had to play doh, me, soh, doh, reaching top 'G' in one rapid sweep, the high note not being easy to reach even for a person with some skill.

They were now singing Grace, and I had further time to ponder on the possibilities. What if I had to sound the 'advance'? This was sometimes used when the dining-hall wasn't being cleared fast enough and the pace had slowed down to a walk. It was the call cavalry used when they advanced, and when the stirring notes rang out in the hall it brought forth the instantaneous shout from all hands of 'charge', and there would be a concerted rush for the door. It was at this stage that I was saved any further doubts, as the proper bugler arrived just in time to sound the 'carry on'.

I discreetly mingled with the crowd as they doubled out, thanking my lucky stars that I had been saved at the last moment.

Chapter Fourteen

COLD WEATHER

JACK HAD NOW REACHED THE AGE when he became a full member of the band. He took his place on my left both in the band-room and in marching order, and had now become a very proficient player. There were two other boys, one played the euphonium, the other the baritone, and with three double-bass players, we were now quite strong in what was usually a rather weak section. Our bandmaster selected and arranged more marches which had stirring bass solos and long melodies for the euphonium, and when occasion arose, as when we marched through the City, we really made a good show and drew large crowds. My instrument could produce a loud brassy tone, similar to a trombone or French horn, and on occasions would blare away to give additional power, but when the euphoniums had a softer, more melodious part, I could tone it down to suit the mood. It was the same when we played at our many engagements or at our Saturday dances. My instrument suited the popular ragtime and jazz which sometimes required the loud, brash sound, and I delighted in giving it the full strength, but my most pleasant memories are when I accompanied the euphoniums.

Jack and I were now firm friends. He was turning out to be a very smart lad, meticulous about his dress, and I always found him fair and considerate. We would engage in some friendly horseplay when we were in the band-room and Corporal Swift was in charge, especially when we were cleaning our instruments. There would be sentences, loud enough to be overheard, which included 'Bootnecks, leathernecks, last in first out' (a skit on first in last out), etc., or a reference to the 'cheap' Woodbines he smoked, which sometimes ended with a light cuff on the ear. But things were kept well within reason. I remember Jack once went up to him with assumed innocence and asked, 'Do you think one Player is worth two Woodbines, sir?' Corporal Swift seeing the point, but expertly changing it to our disadvantage replied, 'If I catch you with either I'll see your arses warmed, m'lads.'

We spent most of our spare time either reading or walking endless miles up and down the well-worn path under the trees. Winter or summer, even in the fog, we would walk and talk about what we did on our last leave and what we would like to do on our next—camping out in a tent, then almost unknown except for the Boy Scouts, different types of tents we might be able to make (buying óne was outside of our imagination), what we would be able to cook, or the possibility of catching a rabbit perhaps. The ideas were fanned into white heat after reading books like *The Swiss Family Robinson, Robinson Crusoe,* and the many adventure books of Canadian trappers and explorers of the new-found lands during the 19th century. I was to wait until I left school before I managed to put these dreams into practice.

During bad weather we would very often spend our time in the reading room. This was situated on the southern corner of the gymnasium block and was furnished with desks, like a classroom. It was heated during cold weather, and although it was a reading room and one was expected to take one's own books, there were quite a number of books, including a large set of volumes on 'The World War' (World War One as we would now know it). Surprisingly, these books were kept in good condition considering the room was only supervised by a boy 'librarian' (detached from No. 4 company, I believe). As I have already said, I had a passion for reading and Captain Marryat's books—*Mr. Midshipman Easy, Peter Simple* and *Masterman Ready*—were special favourites. It was also where I often wrote my letters home, wrote up my notes or homework.

Jack remained on the same mess in the dining-hall the whole of his time at the school and, although he did not get made a P.O., he probably got to the top of the table and shared with the captain of the mess the advantage of getting the pick of the meals. The captain of the mess, almost always a P.O., sat at the end of each mess. He did not impose any discipline as such, because everyone was 'off duty' at meal-times, but he did reinforce Sam's commands. There would be sharp cries of 'Quiet' if when the 'G' sounded there was still someone making a noise, but on the whole we were left alone at meal-times. The exception was reading 'deadies' (books), and this was the reason that I made my frequent visits to the Square, one of Sam's regular customers for this 'offence'; I never did realise he had his eye on me all the time.

The captain of the mess's main duty was to see to its smooth running by detailing the 'cooks' of the week each Sunday, and to see that they prepared the meals and carried out their proper duties. To get on his 'wrong side' was a sure way to find oneself doing fifth cook for a number of weeks. In the happy event of him being a friend one was assured of good meals while the friendship lasted. His only serving duty was at midday, when he had to collect the 'duff' or 'afters'. He very often delegated this task to his 'first hand' who sat opposite him, on whose return he apportioned it out to be passed down each side of the table. He was, no doubt, responsible for the cleaning up of the mess, but the only occasion I remember him staying behind was to give moral support when we went after the cake.

Once one was made a P.O. one's troubles were over as far as work and food were concerned, and one received a small payment each month into the bargain, which was usually recommended by the schoolmaster, and had to be confirmed by the company officer who forwarded it on for approval.

On being appointed a second-class petty officer one would assist in supervising in the dormitory, taking charge of the scrubbing party under punishment in the evenings, until one became used to the job, and then one took charge of small groups or stations. Eager to shine and make a good impression, some of them made life difficult, and for the younger boys and those whom they had made a 'mark' of, they could make life a misery.

On being promoted to first-class one took a more responsible position, sometimes supervising several second-class P.O.s or a larger 'station'; even the whole company would at times come under one's command. This was mainly possible when the chief was absent and there were a number of other P.O.s doing duty as captain of the mess at the dining-hall.

Petty officers came chiefly in two main categories. There were the 'crushers' who led everyone a dog's life—the P.O.s as well as the rest of us. Some of them being in the seamanship class, carried a short length of thick rope which they continually fashioned intricate knots, Turk's Heads, Matthew Walkers and Manrope Knots, which made excellent 'stonickys' and they were therefore quite justified in walking around twirling these painful weapons as they could always say they were practising their knots. The other group consisted mainly of older boys who were more concerned with concentrating on their studies and just making sure things ran along satisfactorily without too much disturbance to anyone.

It can be seen that these boys in office determined the kind of life we led, and it must be taken into consideration that a company of a hundred or so boys up to the age of 15½ had to be kept under control. That some dozen or so boys of the same age did so shows the high standard of discipline that was instilled in one from the beginning. I was recommended for P.O. twice during my time at the school, but the recommendation did not go the whole course. In fact, there were few P.O.s in the band; perhaps we did not spend enough time with our companies to justify being put in a position of command.

The first, second class and Chief Petty Officers (C.P.O.s) under the company officer's supervision, ran the company. It was the C.P.O. who took command whenever the company mustered, either on the parade ground or in the gymnasium. It was he who drilled his company into a smart unit and, with the second-class, made sure that everyone was neat and tidy before reporting to the company officer that all was correct, and he in turn reported to Lieut.-Commander Yeo that his company was properly dressed and ready for whatever activity was to take place.

The 'chief' was always 'stationed' in the dormitory where he reigned supreme. He was usually to be found on or around his 'stand' in the company of one or two of his P.O.s. (A boy was detailed to keep the 'stand' clean and polished, to make the bed and generally act as an orderly.) I am not sure whether the chief actually worked out the details of manning the various 'stations' weekly, or whether it was a joint effort between company officer and chief—it was probably the former with the company officer vetting it before Sunday evening when the instructions were read out.

The company officers, all ex-Navy men, had the dual role of looking after their company and acting as instructors in the seamanship classes. They were, without doubt, specialists in their field and, although untrained in any teaching methods, instilled their teachings into their pupils firmly and permanently. In the role of company officer they ruled from a distance, and nearly all supervision was delegated to the petty officers. From 'wakey-wakey' in the morning when the gas-lights were turned up, morning prayers and divisions, muster for meals, distribution of the mail before 'skirmish', at wash lavatory in the evening and at bedtime when he dimmed the lights, the C.O. or his 'stand in' would be with the company.

He would be in the dormitory the first thing on Saturday mornings when the beds were pushed aside and half the floor was thoroughly polished, and he would visit the other stations at intervals to see that all was well. Living close to the dormitory he was always available should the need arise, and working closely with the chiefs and P.O.s he was always aware of what was going on.

When beds were 'made up for Saturdays', mattresses and pillows, as well as the clean linen for the following week, were exposed for inspection. Each article was folded with the boy's number showing so that it could be ascertained that everyone had a complete kit, in good condition, that it was marked properly and not likely to be lost in the wash. The company officer would go round during the day and there would be a large 'deck party' that night if things had not been satisfactory.

The last weeks of 1928 were bitterly cold. Heavy snow had fallen on several occasions and hard frosts had lasted for some days. There were several slides on the parade ground which, taking advantage of the high ground near the colonnade, enabled one to slide almost the whole distance to the gulley at the opposite side. With the continual traffic of hundreds of feet tramping to the top of the slope, these 'paths' became slippery, and the whole area was like glass. It was impossible to hold divisions or to march-past so, on Sunday, inspection was held in the gymnasium where the 'Skipper' took the opportunity to tell us that from then on sliding was forbidden. After each fall of snow, snow-fights took place, and I saw one brave hit 'Yeo'y' on the back of the neck. He took it in good part, without taking any apparent notice and walking straight on to the Queen's House; but he commented on it the next morning at divisions.

In the band we suffered considerably from cold hands; our instruments felt like blocks of ice. It suddenly dawned on me that during my visits to the office (I had to go there every three weeks to apply for local leave), I had seen a shelf bearing the label 'Found', on which were a few articles, including gloves. I put my idea to Jack. He thought it a good one providing I was the one to go in first, for to begin with we would settle for just the one glove, and if it came to the worst, share it. 'Has anyone found a left-hand glove?' I asked, not wishing to tell an outright lie and say I had lost one. 'What colour?' 'Navy blue', I replied, knowing that it had to be that, black or dark brown to be uniform. 'Did you say left or right hand?', he continued. 'Left', I replied. One could always stop playing and blow on the fingers of the right hand, but could not let go of one's instrument with the left. 'Look over there', the chief company officer said at last, nodding towards the shelf. Lost would not be the appropriate word for the description of the gloves, discarded would be far more accurate. I gave a quick glance at the few gloves, sorted out the left hands and selected the best. 'This is the one, sir', I said, waving it as I walked out.

He must have been somewhat surprised a short while afterwards when a second boy went through the same performance. Now the great defect in this scheme was that there was a finger missing on each of the gloves, and while we were prepared to darn a fair-sized hole, or re-make the top of a finger, a whole one was far beyond our capabilities. After some discussion it was agreed that another visit would have to be made by each of us in turn to obtain a glove with the required digit to cover the one that was missing. After a few days we made our second visit.

By now we knew more or less what stock was available for the right hands, and after we had thought a suitable time had elapsed, made another appearance at the office. But by this time I sensed that there was a growing suspicion in the C.C.O.s mind that there was a pair of apparently absent-minded boys in the school who would benefit from a touch of the cane to stop them losing things, so we gave it up for the time being.

A sharp-eyed bystander, watching when we marched to church, might have noticed two boys in the front row of the band each having a glove on the left hand with a finger of a different colour protruding through, and on the right hand, the glove may or may not have been a different colour—but one thing was certain, at least one bare finger would be poking through.

It became so treacherous underfoot that it was impossible both to march and play an instrument; in fact it was almost impossible to march. We manfully set off one morning on our Wednesday 'march out'. We carried our instruments but did not play them, everyone being kept in step by a regular beat 'on the side drum. We were only a few yards away from the gate in Romney Road when our drum-major slipped and measured his length on the floor, his busby and mace flying up the road, much to the amusement of the rest of the school. He got up and finished the march, although he was shaken and bruised. The next morning I saw Corporal Swift viewing the smashed silver crown on what was reputed to be Queen Anne's walking stick with some concern. It had to be sent to the silversmith for repair.

At last Christmas leave arrived, and we still had the cold weather with us. On leave morning we mustered on the parade ground with our instruments, but again the ground was too slippery for us to play. All was ready, the order 'quick march' was given, and we started off. When they realised that the band wasn't going to play, the boys burst into song, singing the tunes we would have played. They certainly made more noise. 'Goodbye Greenwich' rang out as we carefully marched down the Romney Road. I was more concerned about slipping and smashing my instrument than anything else. 'There's No Place Like Home' was now being sung. When we had played this on previous leave mornings I had been too busy playing to think of the words, but now a lump came to my throat. How nice the word 'home' sounded, and did I imagine it, or was it sung a little softer than the previous march?

Chapter Fifteen

SPRING TERM 1929

AT THIS STAGE OF THE STORY I have the advantage of having kept a diary for the year 1929 but, as one might imagine, in a routine that does not vary much from week to week, or year to year, the entries are all very similar. Every Sunday one reads, 'Church, wrote home'; now and again there is an addition 'Band went to . . . engagement', or on the Sunday before each leave, 'Walking Sunday', or to break the monotony, 'rained all day'.

It was to be the last complete year for me at the school, and there were to be many changes and highlights before the year's end. Without giving a day-to-day record, or even a week-to-week, I will now and again give dates where I think it desirable to clarify the story.

I was now attending seamanship classes on one morning of each week in the seamanship classroom. This was situated at the southern end of the gymnasium, next door but one to the reading room and opposite the large bathing pool. It was a large room containing several working models of ships, machinery, equipment and gear, which enabled the boys to practice on a smaller scale, what many of them would be called on to do when they were in the Navy (see plate 38).

Along one wall there was a stout spar, hinged to the wall at one end, and with a wire stay which stretched from the top of the wall to the other end. When this was swung out and held in position by guys fore and aft, a rope ladder, fashioned with an eye at the bottom, was lowered from the outer end of the boom. This was used by a crew coming alongside a ship in a boat to get inboard, and, assuming we were in a boat and had made fast to the eye in the 'Jacob's ladder', we scrambled up along the boom, holding onto the wire stay, until we were 'inboard', from where we jumped down to the floor again. This model, except for length, was almost full size. There were also two large model ships and a fore-end section, the ships being about fifteen feet long, and the bow section about ten feet long. Each was designed to enable a particular kind of drill to be practised, or exercise explained.

For the first weeks it was 'anchors and cables', and for this the large bow section of a ship was used. It was a replica of the forecastle of a battleship, complete with the three anchors stowed up tight in the hawse-pipes. These were lowered and raised, using the cable holders and capstans. We became more familiar with names that we had learned at evening classes— 'Blake's screw stopper', 'Senhouse slips' and 'swivel pieces' were now being handled. Moving to one of the ships one day, we moored 'fore and aft', moving the model around on wheels to the desired position. I eventually passed my test ('passed out') on this subject, although it was not one of my favourites.

A model that we all wanted to operate was the one used for 'compass and helm'. It was rather a crude affair to look at, a platform roughly in the shape of a ship, in that it was pointed at one end and rounded at the other. It was about ten feet long and nine inches off the ground, and had a short mast with three yards, on which hung two limp sails. The main features, however, were a full-size binnacle and steering-wheel. One got 'aboard' and stood at the 'helm'; an instructor stood on the floor alongside.

The instructor would give a course to steer, then alter it to a different reading. Having been thoroughly taught the theory, it was a simple matter to spin the wheel until the 'ship' was on course. The model turned to the desired direction as the wheel was turned, and one could soon be caught out letting the 'ship' drift off course when the instructor, unseen by the 'helmsman', applied a little 'wind and current' with his foot.

On another large model of a warship we would lower and hoist the boats from their davits (it was all done by hand in those days), and the larger boats like the steam pinnace would be 'hoisted out by the main derrick'. This was a large steel boom attached at one end to the main mast by a huge 'hinge', and hoisted and lowered by wire topping lifts, and massive wire purchases. These were powered from motors, but the tackles for swinging inboard and outboard were by hand. Of course there were no cranes on board in those days.

These lessons described in a few lines did in fact, take many weeks, and there were other subjects that would have to be studied during the next 12 months—'buoys and beacons', 'rule of the road at sea', 'morse and semaphore', all of which by now I had some considerable knowledge, though it was the practical side that we were, as far as possible, to learn.

'Curly' took the class for knots and splicing, and sometimes during the lesson would tell us of his life as a boy before the mast on a 'windjammer' and, later, in the Navy. We listened intently as he told us of the voyages he had made and the many ports he had visited all over the world. It was during these lessons that the real 'Curly' became apparent. When the façade of bluster had finally dropped he was a kind and patient tutor.

It continued bitterly cold, and on Wednesday 6 January, I wrote, 'Inch and a half of snow, usual March Out'. By the beginning of February it was so cold that we were unable to play our instruments out in the open as the valves froze. Every morning, at eight o'clock in the summer and nine in the winter, the band had to attend 'colours', when the Union Jack was hoisted on the flagstaff on the roof of the Queen's House, and the band played the National Anthem. For the previous few weeks we just marched out to the stern of the 'ship' and stood to attention when the clock struck nine, the flag was hoisted, and we then returned quickly to the band-room to thaw out.

On Monday, 11 January, I recorded 'The coldest day for twenty years', and on the 13th, laconically, 'Cold bath, March Out, Bugle Band played'. On Thursday, 14th, 'Herrings for breakfast—frozen, the vinegar was lumps of ice'. It was a hard time, especially for me, for my 'station' was 'windows' during this, the coldest week of the year.

All was not gloom at this time, however, for we were to have great improvements in our diet. It was decided that we should have more daily milk, and this was to be issued on one day at teatime instead of tea, and on the following morning the cocoa would be made entirely with milk. At the same time there was

an increase in our supper issue of cheese. When we had ship's
biscuits ('doggies') for supper in the future, they would be
augmented by Cheddar cheese. The menu for suppers now read:

Sunday	Bread and cheese
Monday	Biscuits and cheese
Tuesday	.Currant bread
Wednesday	Bread and cheese
Thursday	Biscuits and cheese
Friday	Currant bread
Saturday	Biscuits and cheese

The following week we were surprised to find an egg
('whistler') each on the breakfast table, with a promise of one
each fortnight. On the next Tuesday, instead of the hated
'Irish stew', we were now served with proper Irish stew with
pearl barley and dumplings. This was to be served alternately
with real 'moggie pie' with rabbit instead of beef. In a month
our diet had really changed for the better.

We also did well for entertainments during this period, for
we had a lantern lecture on 'Old London' at the end of January,
and in February went to the Greenwich *Hippodrome* to see
' "Q" Ships', as well as our annual visit to the pantomime at
the *Lyceum* theatre, where we saw 'Beauty and the Beast'.
The occasion was made even more interesting for me when
the band, who had the privilege of being seated in the stalls,
was invited 'back stage' during the interval. We were shown
around the dressing-rooms, the scene-shifting arrangements
were explained, and we were generally fussed over by the
actors and actresses. The highlight of the occasion was when
a cameraman appeared and we posed for our pictures to be taken
on the stage amid the scenery. We were at first grouped with
the leading artists, then with various sections of the company,
and then the whole cast. It was all very exciting. The pictures
appeared in the daily papers on the following day, and I
managed to see a well-thumbed copy some days later.

My third badge was awarded this term, as I had been at the
school for two years and four months. Life had become considerably easier. Because of my commitment to the band, the
number of 'stations' that I could be employed on was limited.
Jobs that did not require regular attendance, such as 'windows'

and 'paintwork', were quite common as they could be dropped at any time when my services were required elsewhere.

There was the odd occasion when I took the place of the captain of the mess when he was absent, in one period during 1929 I was doing this duty for two weeks. There were other occasions when I would take charge of a small squad on some minor duty, such as a section of the laundry, on a Saturday morning. It was all better than doing the work oneself, especially if one was going to be harassed while doing so.

I had also become better orientated in the relationship between living in the school and the outside world. For the first six months or so I had thought of myself as cut off from the outside world, like being on some remote island. As time went on the invisible barrier between the inside of the school and the town of Greenwich began to blur, and school and home took on a different relationship. For the first few terms, I viewed home and leave as some distant dream that was far, far away, but now the regular sequence of leave and school was clearer. This might have been due to the fact that I went out on local leave every three weeks and therefore each term was broken down into periods of waiting of less than a month. I notice in my diary that I went on local leave three times during this term, each on a Wednesday, and on each occasion returned at six o'clock in time to see the weekly pictures, instead of returning at seven thirty when the leave expired. It is therefore apparent that the desire to be outside the gates until the very last minute had somewhat abated, although my heart always dropped a little as I entered. Both Jack and I were very fortunate to be able to take this leave, which was only allowed because my aunt lived so near, and we were two of the very few with this privilege. For the great majority, it was an unbroken stretch of confinement from one leave to the next and, for quite a few, from the time they joined until they left. For those who were left behind during the leave period, there were organised outside trips, but of course these could not be compared with the freedom of being on leave.

It was about this time of the year when we had one of the periodic epidemics of influenza. It spread rapidly and the infirmary was soon overwhelmed. The Upper Nautical (No. 9) company was moved to Trafalgar quarters, and the hundred or so beds were quickly filled with the victims. The doctor and nurses worked flat out on these occasions, as there was no additional staff available. It was a case of a quick turnover of patients. Those in bed were liberally dosed with quinine after the initial dose of 'Black Jack' or 'White mixture' and, as soon as the patients' temperatures dropped and they were able to get out of bed, they had to assist with the distribution of meals. At the earliest opportunity, although not before they were fit, they were discharged to make way for the newcomers; there was no room for convalescence.

Now and again there was a small outbreak of scarlet fever or, worse still, diphtheria, when the victims and their close contacts were rushed off to the Infectious Diseases Hospital at Shooters Hill. We were involved in a test when some hundred or so boys were inoculated with a serum which claimed to be a prevention against these two diseases. I was one of the guineapigs, and I have still got the small mark on my wrist. It was evidently successful because, after a suitable time, it was given to the remainder of the school. Much later it became part of the national policy.

It was getting near to the time when we would have to get a 'civvy' haircut, or be caught out and have our hair 'cropped' just before going on leave. For some unknown reason (perhaps it had been on a Wednesday afternoon when we had our local leave and it was early closing day), the barber shop was closed. This was a disaster of the first magnitude, and when we returned to the school that evening it seemed that there was no alternative but to let things take their course, and to hope that we would pass unnoticed for the rest of the term.

I went to bed that night trying to think of a way out of this difficulty. I could get my aunt to bring in comb and scissors and we could try and do it ourselves, but it seemed doubtful that we would be able to do the job to the company officer's satisfaction. In the end it became apparent that there was only one solution, 'over the wall'. Having decided on this, the next question was, 'How?' It is strange when I look back that I did not take Jack into my confidence. If I did, the idea did not meet with his approval or co-operation, for this was strictly a one-man affair.

I did not go into it lightly for, if caught, the punishment was six of the best, which was so severe that it was to be discontinued in the Services in the near future. To quote Dr. Samuel Johnson, 'Nothing sharpens the wits of the felon more than the sight of the hangman's rope', and numerous ideas were thought of and rejected before I finally went to sleep. The next morning the problem was still being pursued; one thing had, however, been decided. The two well-known places, the old observatory and the wall by the rifle range which led into the old churchyard, were out of the question, because too many boys had been caught there. I thought of some improbable ways of crossing the colonnade, over the low iron railings, across the narrow garden into the park beyond; impossible, but at last, during the day, the idea formed and built up.

I remembered the door in the wall at the rear of the infirmary that I had first noticed when I had spent some two weeks in bed with poisoned fingers. It had the advantage that one would appear to be attending the surgery until one arrived right at the door, and then quickly one could slip through the passageway to the outside wall, and through the door, which was only two hundred yards from the barbers.

Next I had to decide on the time. One would be missed least from the time when we finished our work at eight in the morning until nine o'clock when lessons and the daily work began. Surgery also started at eight thirty, and if one was to be asked the reason for such an early appearance in the hospital grounds, one could complain of an acute pain in the stomach— at the worst it would only be a dose of 'Black Jack'.

The next morning I could hardly eat my breakfast, for fear and excitement. Fortunately, I had a 'station' near to the gymnasium, and was also able to get away shortly before eight o'clock. I hurriedly changed into my No. 2 blue suit so as to be ready for school on my return, and hastened out of the gym., across the short distance to the gate that led into the hospital gardens (the new nurses' home was being built on this site at the time), and made my way along the gravel path as quickly as I dared. I was making good time as it was only just past eight o'clock, but my heart sank lower and lower as I reached the point of no return, the surgery door.

I gave a quick look round, darted the few yards to the next
doorway and, while in the short passageway, stopped for a
few moments to get my breath back and to have second
thoughts. With heart pounding I crept stealthily forward,
under the cycle-shed to the door. Gently turning the brass knob
I pulled. The door, to my surprise, opened, and in a moment
I was outside.

My legs took me the short distance across the road, round
the corner to the barber shop. There was not a soul in sight.
Breathlessly I reached the door only to find that the shop had
not yet opened. In desperation I rang the bell and rattled the
door; there was no reply. I waited a few moments. I could not
waste time hanging around so I gave the door another good
shake. This commotion was interrupted by a gentle tap on the
collar. 'What are you after, son?' I spun round as if I had been
shot, to see that it was a small, middle-aged lady who had made
the enquiry.

'I am after a haircut', came the astonishing reply.

'What, this time of the morning?' she replied, her voice
rising to a falsetto with incredulity. 'The shops are not yet
open.' I then realised that the early hours we took for granted
in the school weren't shared by the local barbers outside, and
that my risk had been for nothing. My thoughts were interrupted by her words, 'You had better be getting back to the
school, son; I work in the infirmary, and you can come back
with me'. My heart sank down to my boots. 'If she is one of
the "nurses" ', I thought, 'I am as good as outside the Skipper's
office tomorrow morning.'

'I'll show you the way back', she said. 'Over the road and
through that door', little knowing that it was the one I had
just come out of, nor did I think it prudent to tell her. As we
made our way back she told me that she was one of the
cleaners (see plate 25), and as she entered through the door she
made sure that the coast was clear before she let me in. I gave
her a grateful 'Thank you' as I left her.

During the day I could not concentrate on my work,
what with the excitement of the morning, and the knowledge
that I must go through the same ordeal again if I was to avoid
having my hair shorn before going on leave. As the day wore

on I decided that my next try would be that evening. Surgery was at six o'clock, directly after we had washed. Boys would be going to their various evening classes dressed in their No. 2 blue suits. I would mingle with them and then join those sauntering along to the hospital and, at the last moment, slip away through the passage as before.

My plan went without a hitch. Directly I got outside, the traffic and the passers-by gave me confidence. I walked into the barbers and sat down among those awaiting their turn. I watched the scissors snipping away with some impatience, and in a short time the barber finished the customer in the chair, who then stood up to be brushed down. 'Next gent, please', said the barber, looking around. One of the men started to get up off his chair. 'I think this young gent is in a hurry, you don't mind him going next?' He looked around the room with a knowing smile, and gave a wink to the customer who should have been next, who resumed his seat. I sprang quickly into the chair, he tucked the sheet around my shoulders and started to snip. 'Put your collar on next time, lad', he whispered. He knew what I had overlooked; no-one would have been allowed out of the school improperly dressed, and there was I without collar or cap. However, all went well and I returned unobserved. I entered the gym and searched for Jack. 'Look', I said, 'hair cut.'

The Spring term ended with the shattering news that I, with two others, was to be relegated to class four. This was a real blow, for to get back to class two again would not be easy as it had to be made in one go. I went on leave in a very sombre frame of mind. My diary records, 'Took Home Five Shillings and Sixpence'. I must have been a spendthrift during that term, as I was then getting two shillings a month 'band pay'.

Chapter Sixteen

SUMMER TERM 1929, OLYMPIA

MY MEMORIES OF CLASS FOUR are very vague; I cannot even remember the master's name. There is, however, one faint picture that remains. I am sitting at my desk, the sun is streaming in through the window, and I am busy at a geography lesson. I swear to myself that I will get back into class two come what may. Perhaps the hardest blow was the realisation that now the possibility of getting eventually to class one was very remote, if not impossible. The mathematics seemed to me to be at an especially low standard compared with what I had been used to, and I missed some of the more advanced subjects that were excluded from this class. The only thing I could do now was to really get down to study.

One of our first engagements this term was, with the remainder of the school, to form guard of honour for the Duchess of York when she opened the new wing at Miller's Hospital, Greenwich. It was Tuesday, 14 May, a bright, sunny day and we marched the fairly short distance from the school to the hospital entrance where we formed-up on each side of the road. From the entrance to the hospital building the nurses lined the route. It wasn't long before the duchess arrived, and walked slowly between the ranks. She was called the 'Smiling Duchess', and how gracious she seemed as she paused and spoke to one or two of the boys, and then to several of the nurses as she passed. She finally entered the main doorway and, our part of the proceedings now over, we marched back to the school. Later we had the pleasure of seeing our photographs in the local newspaper.

The highlight of this term was the inclusion of a contingent of boys and the band in the military tattoo at the Olympia. We had only been back from leave for a few days when the band began to practise music for 'our engagement on 23 May'.

163

During this time volunteers were called for throughout the school, and on Friday, 19 April, one week after our return, some two hundred boys and the band assembled on the parade ground. The gymnasium instructors supervised the group and formed them up into five columns facing the 'ship'. The band took its usual place on the parade backing onto the 'ship', facing them.

When all was in order, 'Yeo'y' came out of the office and walked smartly to the front of the columns, and after a quick look along the ranks, told us of the forthcoming engagement.

> After the success of the party that went to Deauville last year it has been decided that we will take part in the Annual Military Tattoo at the Olympia this year, commencing 23rd May. A hundred and fifty or so boys will be needed, so fifty or so of the present company will have to drop out. It is up to everybody to be on his toes and put everything into it. We will be performing a shortened version of the Hornpipe, and a display of Cutlass Drill, the same as the Deauville Party did, and the boys who made that trip and are still at the School will be included in this year's team.

'Yeo'y', one could see, was highly delighted with this operation and had already instilled a sense of excitement and eagerness into the boys.

Whenever there was to be an event at the school there were always endless preparations. A visit from a celebrity or a civic occasion would incur hours of drill and practice. This was going to be the last word in practice. For the first two weeks it was every other day, the last one of which, I wrote in my diary, 'Was filmed by the Movietone News, the new Talking Pictures', and from then on it was every day except Saturdays and Sundays. At first the band had little to do. We played when the hornpipe was being practised, but as all the boys already knew the steps it was only a matter of polishing things up, and culling those not up to standard. During the cutlass drill the band had nothing to do as each stage of this was by word of command, and I believe at Olympia was carried out in silence except for a blast on the whistle to commence.

On the Monday of the fourth week we shifted the emphasis from the static drill to marching. Making our entry 'into the arena', the band led the five columns, then wheeled away and turned to take up positions similar to those on the parade ground, only now we were at the rear. At the conclusion of the performance we wheeled to the left, and the remainder at the appropriate time joined up behind to march out as one unit again.

There wasn't enough space on the parade ground for these manoeuvres so we now practised in the park. It was now the band who did most of the work, not playing at first but concentrating on the marching and taking up positions. The responsibility for this part of the operation fell to a great extent on the drum-major for the band, when playing and marching, focus most of their attention on their music. Those in the front rank could see him at a glance and the rest followed on.

This led to an amusing, though in the end a painful, incident. We were going through the whole programme and it was just a matter of the final timing and polish. However, things had not been going well on this particular morning, and 'Yeo'y' was stamping around and the instructors were shouting.

We had 'marched into the arena' with the band playing, and we were about to break away and turn from the column. We were blaring away and the time had come for us to start turning to the left. For some unaccountable reason the drum-major held the mace out at arm's length to his right, and the four players in the front row started to turn and wheel off to the right. I knew by the stage of the music that we had reached the moment to turn and, automatically, with Jack on my left and with the outside player, wheeled to the left. To add to the confusion, there was a wire about a foot from the ground strung along to indicate the side of the pathway, and the half of the band who had turned to the right were tripping over it. By the time I realised that there was no-one on my right, there were shouts of dismay from all sides. I looked round to see Jack rolling about laughing, and 'Yeo'y', his face dark as thunder, pointing his cane at him and shouting, 'You, outside the Office at nine o'clock tomorrow morning'.

Now it had been a small bone of contention in the past, between Jack and myself, that I had been 'run in' for some small similar 'offence' some time before, and received 'one cut', and that he had still a 'clean sheet', so the thought that we were now going to be even led me impetuously to laugh at him. Immediately 'Yeo'y', seeing me, as he assumed, joining the joke, spun round and shouted, shaking his cane, 'And you.' The next morning, as I made my way to the classroom, rubbing my stinging backside, I ruefully contemplated the fact that the score was still uneven, but it was now two to one.

On Tuesday, 21 May, we went to the Olympia for a full practice before the rehearsal on the following day when the rest of the school as well as a full audience would be present (see plate 31), and on the Thursday the 23rd, we were ready for our first real appearance. King George V had been ill for some time, and was therefore unable to attend, so it was Queen Mary and the Prince of Wales (later Edward VIII) who occupied the royal box on the opening day.

We formed up, just outside the arena, dressed in white lightweight canvas trousers made especially for the occasion, No. 1 blue jumpers, and white caps. The two huge doors started to open. Two three-pace rolls on the drums. We struck up 'A Life on the Ocean Wave' and marched off. The Royal Artillery had just left the arena after giving a demonstration of driving teams of horses pulling guns and gun-carriages, and had churned the ground up like a ploughed field. The first thing I did was to step into a deep rut that the wheels had made and I nearly swallowed my mouthpiece.

There was thunderous applause as we marched to our positions; the performers placed their cutlasses on the ground, on command, and then took one pace backwards to give them enough room to dance the hornpipe. We went through the often-drilled routine and, during the cutlass drill display when the band had nothing to do, I had time to look up at the royal box at the Queen and the Prince. I felt very proud to be so near and playing before them. The boys had now finished the drill and stood to attention, the crowd clapped and roared, and 'Tach', our bandmaster, was impatiently tapping the cuff buttons of his jacket with his baton by flicking it backwards and forwards with his fingers. His normally expressionless face I thought showed a slight sign of pleasure, but he quickly gave a nod to the drummer, and there were the two three-pace rolls, the signal for us to strike up 'Hearts of Oak', and with this stirring march and fired with success, we proudly marched out.

For the next eight days we made the rather long journey daily to do one performance and return immediately to the school. The First Lord of the Air was in the royal box on the second day, the Admiral of the Fleet the next; there was always some notable person to take the salute. For the last five days we gave two performances, one in the afternoon and one in the evening. My diary reads, 'Monday, Lord Mayor of London in the Royal Box; Tuesday, Lord Jellicoe; Wednesday, Princess Royal'; I was getting used to playing before such celebrities.

Between our appearances each day we were able not only to see the remainder of the tournament, but to go round behind the scenes and see the horses and other equipment, and to talk with the other military personnel taking part. We were each served with a glass of milk and rolls for refreshment during this time.

I believe it was on the day that the Princess Royal occupied the royal box that Jack and I decided it would be a good idea to sit in the chair that had accommodated so many famous bottoms. Without more ado, we made our way up the tiers of seats to the front of the box, and it was a work of a moment to jump over the low wall covered with red velvet. Once inside, the question arose, which velvet-covered seat was *the* one? There was no time to hang about so, after a quick conference, it was decided that we would quickly sit on each seat of the front row in turn. My entry for the day reads, 'I went into the Royal Box, sat down on the King's chair'.

At the final performance, on the Friday, the Duke and Duchess of York (later King George VI and Queen Elizabeth) took the salute.

On 22 June the band went on its annual outing, this year to the Regent's Park zoo. It was only an afternoon affair, as we left the school directly after our midday meal. Perhaps it was just as well because it was a very hot day and the smell was rather overpowering at times. We had quite a good time; the highlights of the day were when we were treated to an ice-cream each, and later, to a jolly good tea in the pavilion. We did a certain amount of leg-pulling with Corporal Swift, but it was kept to a very low key as the bandmaster was with us all the time. The fact that we had spent so much time away from the school at the Olympia and at other engagements probably took a lot of the novelty out of the occasion.

It was now time to get down to serious business, for on 5 July the examinations began and I was eager to do well. As I have said before, the senior division only attended classes on alternate days, so we were not subjected to the stress of the remainder of the school who had to go through the ordeal every day, but it was not until the 15th that we finished, and I sat back and eagerly awaited the results.

They came out on the 19th and what a pleasant result it was for me. Top of the class in History and English, and second place overall. There was a ruling that no boy could have more than one prize at a time, so I elected to go for second place in the class. But the biggest prize was that I would now be going back to class two at the beginning of the next term.

As usual, on such occasions, we started practising for prize day on the Monday before this important event, and at the same time my grandfather arrived at Greenwich, for he was staying for the week to attend the prize-giving on the Friday.

On the Tuesday I went and chose my prize, which was a beautifully-bound book with the school crest chased in gold on the front cover. I am afraid in my excitement I wasn't concerned with the title of the book although it was very interesting reading, but took the one that I thought would look the best on a bookshelf. We practised daily until the great event arrived. The stage in the gymnasium was suitably decorated, and there was a long table which extended across the whole width. Seated in the centre was Earl Jellicoe, who was to present the prizes, and on either side sat Admiral Oliphant, Lieut.-Commander Yeo, the headmaster, the doctor, and other celebrities. The boys to receive the prizes were lined up along one side of the gym behind the wall bars, according to their classes.

As each boy received his book, we all eased forward a little until I arrived at the lower step leading up to the stage, then slowly, step by step, to the top. I had just time to have a quick look at the rows of visitors seated below, and to try to get a glimpse of my grandfather when it was my turn to go. Eight paces forward, halt and turn left, two paces forward, a smart salute, take the book in the left hand, shake hands with the great admiral, a murmured thanks, two paces backwards, right turn, and march smartly off the stage. It was all over and I could hear the clapping as I descended the stairs.

Looking back, I realised that I did remarkably well, considering that in the 14½ weeks of this term, I only attended classes on alternate days, and lost time in the long preparation and attendance at the Olympia. Also, I had attended band engagements in places as far away as Croydon and Kensington and, although most of them were at weekends, there was the additional strain of practising for these events as well as the travelling.

At the end of this term I went home in a joyous mood—I had my prize and my prospects in my new class were good. I was well satisfied.

Chapter Seventeen

AUTUMN TERM 1929.   I MISS THE   WATCH

AT THE START OF THE NEW TERM I was very pleased to
return to my old classroom, class two, and although I had
lost my seat in the front row, it was good to be back. In fact
I was seated almost in the back row. When P.D. Woods arrived,
there was soon a casual remark about 'I am glad to see that
one of our Portsmouth friends we thought we had lost is now
back with us'. I felt a warm glow of pleasure at these words
as we commenced work.

Mr. Woods did a lot of teaching from the blackboard and it
wasn't long before I realised that I could not see very clearly
what was being written. I complained to the master, and
within a few days I had to report to the eye specialist at the
Seamen's hospital. The result was that from then on, I had
to wear spectacles in the classroom and when I was reading.

These events made it seem extremely unlikely that I was
going to pass the medical test to enter the Navy in a few
months' time. There was a new scheme of sending boys who
had failed medically for the Navy, on some minor fault, to
Australia or Canada. These two large countries, which then
had only small populations, were seeking educated youngsters
to train for their growing farming and industrial programmes.
From time to time we would see one of these boys, all kitted
up in civilian clothes, come round to say farewell to the masters
and instructors before making his long voyage. It was a good
opportunity, and many of the boys who went were subsequently very successful. I probably gave this some thought,
but I had not yet given up the idea of going into the Navy
at this stage; I just plodded on.

At this time I had developed a passion for football, rather
late in my career in a school, perhaps, where sports counted
well in one's chances of being promoted to petty officer. I

find in my diary at this time, that on most evenings and Saturday afternoons 'I played football'.

The infirmary seems to figure prominently in my working programme. There were several times when I was 'stationed' as 'wards', the duties of which I have already briefly described. The work was mostly dusting around, and polishing the floors with the long-handled polishers. There were tit-bits to be picked up for small services, such as taking messages between patients and their pals back at the school, buying sweets from the canteen or, if one was lucky enough, to be sent outside the school, for fruit and comics. There was hardly any discipline compared with that of the dormitories and similar 'stations', although it paid to keep on the right side of the 'nurses' whom we were supposed to be helping.

Long room orderly's duties were on the ground floor, and consisted mainly of running messages for the doctor and his assistants. I did this duty several times during the last few months before I left the school. The best part of the job was to be sent across to the Seamen's hospital, when it was possible to dawdle along and look at the shops during the short time spent outside the school.

Interspersed with these plum numbers, however, were the less pleasant jobs that came my way, 'gymnasium sweeper', for example, an entry for week commencing 23 September was one instance. This duty required that, each time the gym was cleaned, we had to sweep it from end to end. Each morning wet sawdust was spread all over the floor and we had to sweep it around and then clean it up. On Saturdays the whole area was scrubbed with brooms, and dried with squeegees and floorcloths. The instructors always 'kept things on the move' and I was always thankful when the time came to 'stow brooms'. This Saturday, in spite of the gruelling morning, was a red letter day, for it was the day I received my first monthly payment of four shillings band pay, which was the top rate.

———

For some unknown reason the old-style 'Irish stew' came back onto the menu on Tuesdays. Why this should be so is anyone's guess, as the majority of it was consigned to the waste tins. As a laconic note in my diary reads, 'Irish Stew arrived back; received full Military Honours'.

It was at this point that my training took a new turn. I was in my last six months at the school, and was now considered on 'sea draft'. In the old days, I would have had to live on board the 'ship'; I no longer attended band practice on alternate days with classes, but went to seamanship class instead. My first class was signals, using two flags for the semaphore and one flag or a lamp for morse code. There were about twelve of us altogether, and we were all conversant with both methods. What was now required was practice to achieve a rapid speed of transmitting and receiving messages. One method we used was to form up in pairs, one having the necessary flags, the other a signal pad and pencil. Each pair would take up a position around the parade ground in such a way that although one could see a pair on either side, each could not see the other, so that only one pair would be seen transmitting at a time. The first pair, with the instructor, was usually outside the gymnasium and would send a message to the pair at the bows of the ship, where one would read it out aloud, letter by letter, and the other write it down. At the conclusion of the message, the one who had been writing would pick up the flags and transmit, to the other's dictation, to the second pair, and so on. If the message was in the form of a question, when the answer was returned, each pair would change roles in receiving and sending to give everyone an equal chance.

There was a 32-ft. cutter chocked-up on the gravelled portion of the parade ground, on the east side of the gate, and our next period of instruction was to familiarise ourselves with the construction and handling of the boat. Again, it was a matter of putting into practice lessons that we had previously been taught at evening classes. It was more interesting to see and feel the different parts, especially when we stepped the mast and hoisted the boom and sails. Discipline was eased a little during these lessons and there was time for a little fun, such as 'man overboard' when someone got out of the boat to get something that had been dropped, and a great show of strain when we manned the oars. It was all good fun, and I can still remember the lessons taught after 40 years.

Before leaving the school one had to be able to swim a certain distance clothed in a canvas suit, and it was during one of our seamanship lessons that we were detailed to report to the small swimming bath to carry out this test.

It was a far different atmosphere from that of two years before, when I had knelt shivering on the edge of the bath, waiting to be tipped in, I thought, as I stripped off my clothes and donned the 'duck' suit. We lined up, one behind the other, and the first one dived in. It was really a matter of routine, because all of us were by now good swimmers. At regular intervals we followed, and it was very soon my turn. As I entered the water, I felt the suit immediately pressed tightly against my body, and the strange feeling of being underwater, yet my body being quite dry. As I travelled under the water (as before, I wanted to get as far as I could with the dive) I could feel the water gradually running up the insides of the legs of my trousers and the arms of my jumper. With the first strokes I had become waterlogged and the weight of the suit became apparent and it was increasingly difficult to keep my head above the water. I struggled on, swimming in an almost upright position, and reached the other end; turning, and with a longer actual swimming distance to go, I struck out again, eventually finishing the course. Dripping and panting, we all dried ourselves and dressed and I, for one, hoped that I would never fall overboard and have to swim for very long dressed in that type of suit.

There were three highlights during the week 18–25 October. On Friday, the 18th we celebrated Trafalgar Day with 'foundation pong', after our dinner, followed by a half-day holiday, and on the 25th we celebrated 'Foundation Day' in the same way. The best day of all, however, was the following Monday. It was about 10 o'clock when the master told us to down pens. 'The result of our test on Thursday last', said Mr. Wood, looking around the class. 'The top boy and the winner of the tin of pineapple chunks is our old friend from Portsmouth, Turner'. I could not believe my ears. Top of the class, and so recently in class four. I went to the front of the class, and 'Woody', his sun-tanned face beaming, handed me the prize. 'Of all the many boys who have won this small prize', he said, 'I think giving it to you on this occasion has given me the greatest pleasure'.

A lump came up into my throat. I modestly said 'thank you'. It was my proudest moment at the school. For when I had qualified for my prize in class four, I had the feeling that, as I had previously received a higher standard of education in my other classes than any other of the boys (which, in fact, I had), it was really no outstanding achievement. I had now competed with boys at my own level, and proved that I was not only able to hold my own, but to compete successfully against them.

The question now arose, how were we to open the tin? It was the same evening that I had won the prize, and Jack and I had this problem to solve. The obvious solution, to go to the kitchen and ask for the loan of a tin opener, did not enter our heads. We hunted around for any sharp instrument or railing that had a suitable point, but were unsuccessful; at last, by banging it on the corner of the wall of the gym we made a hole sufficiently large enough to extract the juice. Alas! the fruit had to remain inside, and we reluctantly threw away the tin and contents into the waste bin.

About this time we had a band engagement at Woolwich, for the annual sports day of an internationally-known electrical firm. It was a beautiful day for the time of the year, with bright sunshine, and the luscious green grass made a welcome change to the asphalt and the paving of the school.

We were seated in the same order as was normal on such occasions, and roughly the same order as in the band-room. Jack was on my left, and a boy named Bailey, who played the baritone, on my right. Although Bailey had been sitting next to me in the band-room for about twelve months we had hardly spoken to each other. To talk during practice would invite a sharp tap on the head with a kettle-drum stick and, secondly, there was usually nothing to talk about. He always appeared to be a quiet, rather subdued person, not a brilliant player, but never getting himself punished for bad playing or misbehaving.

The various events, interspersed with our playing of the popular melodies of the day, and a few rousing marches, soon brought the time for the interval near. But just before the last race, and just as we were looking forward to some refreshment, there was an announcement that the next race would be a 'band race'. This, the announcer explained, would start from the bandstand and each one could march in any direction he chose and at the same time he could play whatever tune he preferred. I took a quick look around the ground and noticed that among the obstacles for the obstacle race was a vaulting-horse on the end of which was stuck a black disc. As we descended the wooden steps to the ground, I jokingly said to Bailey, 'There's one of the marks over there, on the horse', and then proceeded to amble aimlessly around, trying to play as I stumbled over the uneven ground. We all wandered around making various noises to the delight of the crowd and, among the cheers, a whistle brought us all to a halt, to select the lucky winner. I wasn't the lucky one, but as we resumed our seats Bailey showed me his left wrist with a new watch strapped to it. 'You were right', he whispered, 'It was on the vaulting horse'. It was unfortunate that for the remainder of the time I was at the school, at each band practice, and in fact each time the band formed up, I was on Bailey's left with the watch in full view.

The Air Force class was formed during this time, to prepare boys who had failed to reach the medical standard required for entering the Navy because of some slight defect in sight or hearing, for the educational entry examination for this new branch of the Services. The boys selected were only from the advance class and classes one and two of the senior division and I (since my eyesight was not up to the required standard), being one of the few selected, was notified that I should report to the new classroom on the following morning. It was a small classroom, at the extreme end of the Upper Nautical classrooms next to the old observatory, and looked out onto the park. It was really part of a room, having a partition which separated it from what was then a stationery store. There were about ten of us in the class, and we seated ourselves one to a desk to await our new master.

He was my idea of a typical Frenchman, his black hair carefully plastered down either side of a central parting, above a rather large Roman nose. He was of medium height, dressed in black. If I remember correctly, he wore either his cap and gown or a kind of dress coat. He soon proved to be meticulous to the point of fussiness, and appeared to be harassed to the state of a nervous breakdown. As to the latter, he might well have been, for his duties were many and varied and included arranging all the educational activities at Trafalgar quarters, including the selective tests to decide which classes the boys would go into when they reached the main school, or if they would qualify for the Upper Nautical school. He also appeared to have other duties concerning the new entries, as he frequently went to and fro to the offices in the Queen's House and the infirmary when the batches of new entries were due to arrive. He seemed to be the custodian of the stationery and, of course, he had to look after us. I say 'look after us' instead of 'teach', because most of our work was now to be revision. We all knew him as Marcus; whether this was his real name or not, I never did find out.

I soon settled down to the new class, and after a few days several things became apparent. Firstly, we were left to our own studies for long periods, often for whole days at a time, while he was employed on his other duties. Secondly, in addition to the class library, there was a very comprehensive collection of books which belonged to the master, which could be read by the class as required. We were also to spend many hours in the science room.

In this class, it was back to the daily class attendance with the addition of further lessons on Saturday mornings, the same hours as the Upper Nautical school. This meant the end of band practice as far as I was concerned and, I am sorry to say, a gradual drift away from it as my studies became more demanding. I, of course, continued to take my place daily, when fortunately the music was familiar, but as time went on and new pieces had to be played it became progressively more difficult. One consolation, however, was that from now on there would be no more scrubbing out of messes, or any job that required a Saturday morning attendance.

Our lessons consisted mainly of working on previous examination papers. What these examinations were for originally I have no idea, but they were mostly well within my capacity and I found life quite pleasant. During the long spells that we were left to our own devices we were allowed to go to the cupboard and select any of the master's books for study after we had finished our allocated tasks. Astronomy, photography, and electronics were his favourite subjects, and we soon found out that if one asked a question selected from one of these, we were in for one or two hours of interesting lecturing to pass the time away.

He spent a lot of his spare time at the Royal Observatory in the park, and would very often tell us of his activities on the previous night. If there was a violent thunderstorm during the night, he would go onto the roof of his home and fix up several cameras. As each flash of lightning exposed the plates, he would replace them in fond hope that he had caught one of them with one of the cameras. Sometimes he would get a result spread over two, or even three, plates, and he would bring the results in and proudly display them on his desk the following morning. One or two appropriate questions, and we could sit back and enjoy an interesting interlude away from our studies.

We spent a lot of our time in the science room, which was situated between the reading and seamanship rooms. Marcus would hand out several books detailing various problems that we would have to solve. They were all to do with mechanics or electricity although, among my first discoveries, was how to make toast with a bunsen-burner and some wire gauze. I soon constructed a gas toaster which was an immediate success, and we had the whole class bringing in their 'stungees' to be baked. What the seamanship class next door thought when the odour of toasting bread began to waft through, I don't know.

I was keenly interested in electronics and, after prevailing upon my aunt to purchase and supply me with copper wire and other bits and pieces, made machines for tapping out the morse code, electric buzzers, coils for giving electric shocks and, later, crystal sets which received the wireless programmes from the London transmitters. It was all very interesting and, as far as the wireless was concerned, advanced, for there were then very few sets available to the public. In fact, when I constructed a three-valve set at home the following year, it was one of the first in the district, and I was hailed as some sort of an alchemist.

Chapter Eighteen

THE LAST TERM

I RETURNED FROM CHRISTMAS LEAVE with mixed feelings. During my leave my mother had not thought very highly of the idea of my joining the Royal Air Force. The popular idea among the residents in my neighbourhood of this young Service was of scatterbrained aristocratic young men, who spent most of their time dashing around the countryside in fast cars, joining the Service for further thrills, and ending up by crashing a 'plane and killing themselves. Looking back, one can quite understand this mentality, for it was during this time that aviation was really making rapid strides, and new records and frontiers were being reached nearly every week; but there were casualties, and the details of flying accidents were only too frequently headline news.

Another reason for her concern was that airmen were sent on long commissions of from five to seven years to the Middle East, to Iran and Iraq, and in those days it was tantamount to being exiled for this long period. The Army also had long commissions with a further disadvantage of being sent to India; the Navy, on the other hand, were usually away for two and a half years.

As the first weeks of the term passed I became more and more unsettled. Here was I, getting on for sixteen years of age; had I been at home I would have been working for the past eighteen months. I was definitely not going into the Navy, the Air Force had lost some of its attraction, and all this study began to seem so pointless. The continual discipline also became irksome, and I neither seemed to belong to the band nor to my company nor to anyone else. I began to wonder where it was all going to end, or whether it was all worthwhile. Jack and I seemed always to be quarrelling, and there would be long periods when we went 'cad' and did not speak to each other. It was all building up towards making the wrong decision when a cool head and a reasonable approach were needed.

Shakespeare's words were certainly true when he wrote:

> There is a tide in the affairs of men,
> Which taken at the flood, leads on to fortune;
> Omitted, all through the voyage of life
> Is bound in shallows and miseries.

I was sitting at my desk, busily engaged in my studies unaware of anything unusual, until I heard my name being called, and looking up I saw that a messenger had arrived and was calling out my name. 'Skipper wants to see you', he said, 'at the double'. It was only a short distance from my classroom along the colonnade to the Queen's House.

I was led into the admiral's study, where he was sitting at his desk. He stood up and came towards me as I entered, and I noticed that the headmaster of the school, dressed in cap and gown, was standing by the window. I cannot remember the exact details of the interview, only that my mother had sent him a letter stating that she had found me employment in Portsmouth and asking for me to be released from the school. The admiral went on at some length on the inadvisability of leaving for such an unpromising start in life, for this was obviously a 'dead end' job, but, directly I heard that there was a possibility of employment and of being able to leave, my mind was made up.

At last he asked me for my opinion. 'I should like to leave, Sir', I replied.

They both spent some considerable time trying to convince me of the foolish step I was about to take. The headmaster stressed the desirability of continuing my studies and the almost certain prospect of my passing the examination, of the terrible conditions outside with millions of unemployed, and the foolishness of taking a job with no prospects. It all fell on deaf ears. All I could see was the opportunity of getting away from the irksome discipline and of earning some money. It was finally decided that I should leave.

Unknown to myself, there was also the problem of clothes. When a boy left to emigrate to Canada or Australia, there were arrangements to kit him out with suitable clothing. When a boy was invalided out, the uniform could be worn for several weeks until he was settled in his new life, when his uniform could be returned. I had no civilian clothes, nor was I likely to be able to get any. I did not think about this problem at the time.

Within a few days I was taken out to the Union Jack club where I was really fitted out. Suit, overcoat, trilby hat (which had just become fashionable), and two each of underwear, with a giant suitcase to carry it all in, except the overcoat which I carried on my arm. I returned to the school to spend what was to be my last night there.

The next morning, after the usual wash and breakfast routine, I went to the dormitory for the last time. I changed into my new clothes, and said farewell to my company officer, who reminded me how lucky I was to be the first one to be so equipped, and went to look for Jack. We had not spoken for several weeks; it was a great pity after we had been friends for so long that when we would be going our different ways, we should have had this unpleasantness. I found him at last, scrubbing the stairs that led from the dining-hall to the scullery. We shook hands, and mumbled a farewell; I don't believe either of us realised that this was to be for ever. We never wrote or saw each other again.

I walked quickly towards the gate and passed through for the last time, turning to the right towards the shops, where I made one or two small purchases. I walked back along the railings; at the gatehouse stood 'Man' Simmons and the two orderlies. They did not recognise me; I was just another civvy. I walked on along past the rails.

CONCLUSION

I have often wondered about the decision made in the Queen's House that sunny spring morning. It was to take me 20 years, until after the war, before I could put my education to good use, but that is another story. Had I continued with my studies and entered the Royal Air Force, would my bones be now resting in some far-off land like those of so many of my school-fellows, or would I have rank and letters after my name?

What benefits were derived from the Spartan training we received at the school, you may ask? The academic education available at that time was very advanced, and there was no limit for those who were able and willing to learn. The success rate of ex-boys in the Navy has always been very high, with a large proportion reaching commissioned and non-commissioned ranks. Even while I was living through the events described in the previous chapters there were two Old Boys carving outstanding careers for themselves.

Admiral Sir Philip K. Enright started his career when he left the school in 1910 and entered the Navy as a boy seaman. Seven years later, four of them served during World War One, was commissioned in the rank of sub-lieutenant. After passing for lieutenant in 1921, his outstanding ability and devotion to duty earned him progressive promotion to command cruisers and battleships. For distinguished services in the Far East during World War Two he was made a C.B.E. Promotion to rear-admiral in 1947 was followed by the award of C.B. in 1949. He was admiral-superintendent at H.M. Dockyard, Devonport, for four years, being reappointed on his promotion to vice-admiral in 1950. In 1952 he was created a K.B.E., and on his retirement in 1953, was promoted to admiral.

Rear-Admiral Sir Sidney Frew, K.B.E., C.B., joined the school in 1903. He left and entered the Navy in 1905 as an

181

engine room artificer (E.R.A.). In 1916 he was appointed as
acting mate (E) soon after joining the battleship *Ajax* based
at Devonport. The following year he was posted to *Mamelook*
(a 34-knot destroyer), and six months later was promoted to
engineer lieutenant.

At the end of 1919 he was aboard *Maidstone* at Portsmouth
for duty with submarines, and this was followed by *Submarine
K12* (noted for her high speed—24.3 knots—over 72 miles*).

For the next three years he was at H.M.S. *Dolphin* (submarine base) with the exception of six months in K14. at the
end of which, in 1926, he was promoted engineer lieutenant-
commander.

The next three years were spent in 'surface ships', and in
June 1929 he was promoted to engineer commander, and as
such served in *Arethusa*, *Sussex* and *Royal Oak*. He resumed his
association with submarines in 1938 when he joined H.M.S.
Medway, in 1939 he was promoted to engineer captain.

After serving 18 months at a torpedo and mine depot, he
returned to *Dolphin*. On 2 January 1945 he was promoted to
engineer rear-admiral and at the end of that year was posted to

*In the year 1915 the Admiralty laid down secretly a class of sub-
marines of revolutionary design. These submersable destroyers as they
were called, were to be the largest, heaviest and fastest submarines built
anywhere in the world at that time; indeed, they proved to be so fast
that no British submarines of 1939–45 could have outstripped them.
They were driven on the surface by steam engines; aft of the conning
towers they carried two retractable funnels. Between August 1916 and
May 1918 the Navy commissioned 17 of the class.

No Class of modern warship in the Royal Navy, or any other navy has
suffered such a calamity as the K. Boats. They were involved in 16 major
accidents and countless smaller mishaps. One sank on her trials. Three
were lost after collisions. A fifth disappeared. Another sank in harbour,
of the 22 built:

K1.   Sank in collision.
K4.   Sank in collision.
K17. Sank in collision.
K13. Sank on acceptance trials, raised and re-numbered K.22.
K5.   Lost on exercise.
K15. Sank in Portsmouth harbour, raised and scrapped.
K18. As M1, sank in collision.
K19. As M2, sank on exercise.

Pembroke as Commander-in-Chief Nore, Admiral of the Fleet Lord Tovey's staff.

He was made a C.B. in 1946, and a K.B.E. in 1949, the same year that he retired. He died on 10 June 1972, and his portrait hangs in H.M.S. *Dolphin.*

It is obvious that he was a man of great qualities, being involved in experimental and often secret work from an early stage in his career. His promotion from lieutenant-commander to commander in three years, especially during the inter-war years when the Navy was being reduced to its lowest capacity, is very remarkable indeed.

In addition to the excellent education, there was physical fitness to consider. Apart from minor hearing and optical defects, largely in the examiner's imagination to keep the intake of the Navy down (the forces were being drastically cut at this time for it was a period of disarmament, and many of the 'failures' joined the Navy a few years later when the requirements of the armed forces were again getting back to normal), there were very few who were not in a very healthy condition.

Then there was the ability to look after oneself. It was soon made apparent, within the first few days, that you had to look after 'number one' or go to the wall. There developed an ability to size-up a situation in a matter of seconds and to decide which course one had to take, an ability to size-up one's fellows after a very brief encounter and decide 'what kind of chap he was'. It was no use trying to 'put one over' on the average Greenwich boy, he was far too wide-awake; in short, one was prepared for the hard outside world when the time came to leave the school.

Respect was another attribute. 'Fear God and Honour the King' was more than a slogan. In fact one can safely say, Greenwich boys were prepared to take their places in the world as men, in the best sense of the word.

Unfortunately, a high proportion of Old Boys were killed during the two World Wars, especially World War Two, when it was the far-from-adequate regular Navy that bore the brunt of the attack until sufficient ships were built and men trained to turn the tide. Time and time again, the same men and ships were in action (especially on escort duties) so that it was usually only a matter of time before one's ship became a casualty, with its quota of loss of life.

The standard of education seems always to have been very high. Lessons taught 50 years ago remain fresh in my mind. An old Boreman boy, at the time of writing, nearing his nineties, writes, 'Looking back over the years, I have often marvelled at the method of teaching because the subjects were so instilled into our brains that it remained in the mind for life, in my case seventy odd years so far'. It is all the more amazing that the company officers who taught seamanship had no experience at all of teaching, and yet again, the knowledge was placed firmly and was there to stay.

Of course, not all the boys aspired to great academic heights but, besides education, they acquired physical fitness, loyalty and comradeship, the prime benefits of which I do not believe were surpassed by boys or girls in any other establishment anywhere.

VOCABULARY

'Birthday bunce'—bumping one on one's birthday.
'Bird' or 'fowl'—Silly boy.
'Bore have'—I'll have. (Bore have first pick).
'Bust up'—feast or meal.
'Blowey'—small.
'Bollicky'—water jug.
'Brick'—to be afraid.
'Corno'—corned beef.
'Crop'—school haircut.
'Cheese cutters'—creases in trousers.
'Cadder's Eve'—Friday before leave.
'Cheesers'—socks.
'Currant toke'—currant bread.
'Cur'—crust.
'Chin', 'Jew' or 'Shonk'—miser.
'Cheddar'—cheese.
'Duff bag'—white cap cover.
'Deadies'—books.
'Dips'—drinking basins.
'Dip'—bathe.
'Dip, have a'—go to the swimming pool.
'Doggies'—biscuits.
'Dosh'—to steal.
'Fancies'—tapes for tying the black silk.
'Flannel front'—false flannel front piece made of white and of lighter material than navy flannel.
'Foundation pong'—highly spiced pudding served on Foundation Day and other special occasions.
'Fat dobs'—bacon.
'Fat wang'—meat.

'First pick'—choose first. One who calls it first. Get first choice.
'Fudge'—wear badges one was not entitled to.
'Flippo'—boy with large ears.
'Flop'—margarine.
'Go cad'—break friendship, have a row.
'Gibbey'—hat or cap.
'Get over wall'—break bounds.
'Geasers'—badges.
'Home'—hospital.
'Home, up'—in hospital.
'Halvies'—share.
'Hog'—greedy boy.
'Jippers'—gravy.
'Jossey'—a boil.
'Keeping back'—not sending items to the laundry, or boots to repair.
'Kick'—expulsion.
'Knackers'—knock-kneed.
'Leave cash day'—day before leave (Tuesday).
'Lay or lie in'—stay in bed.
'Lug up'—study.
'Lecture'—make a speech or a talk.
'Licker'—one who tries to gain favour with those in authority.
'Lugs'—ears.
'Lash out'—hurry up.
'Man'—Mr.
'Mess shelf'—to be at the mess shelf end or the lower end of the mess.
'Milky cocoa'—cocoa made with milk.

'Moggie pie'—rabbit or beafsteak pie.

'New Jacks'—new entries.

'Nozzer'—nosey person.

'Nurses'—women employees.

'Nimbles'—leather slippers worn by P.O.s.

'Narkey'—jealous, envious.

'Out in town'—on local leave.

'Oxing in, Oxer'—one who pushes in a queue out of turn.

'Old Jack'—boy with over two years in the school. Three badges.

'Orderly'—messenger.

'Pluck'—bully.

'Pass out'—qualify.

'Peck'—nose, or boy with a large nose.

'Pull up'—to get caught out, to be told off.

'Quiff'—hair left a little longer at the forehead.

'Spinnage'—cabbage.

'Spud'—potato.

'Spud machine'—potato cleaning machine.

'Stungee'—portion of bread, usually half a loaf, cut into sandwiches so that all the slices fit back into the original shape of the loaf.

'Saving a place'—line up in a queue for someone until he arrives.

'Scrub out'—scrub mess table, stool and floors.

'Scrub decks'—polish floors (dormitory), usually as a punishment.

'Stonicky'—short piece of rope or spliced leather boot laces used as a weapon to urge the boys to greater effort. The former often had a large knot formed in the business end.

'Skirmish'—marching across the grounds in long lines picking up paper, etc.

'Scheming'—idling or shirking.

'Spinning up'—talking.

'Stripey'—one with three badges.

'Snotter'—handkerchief.

'Spare'—'Any surplus?' 'Let me have what you don't want.' A silent question by pulling out the skin under the chin.

'Scrag'—to beat up.

'Spit'—cigarette end.

'Squeegee'—boy with thick lips.

'Stinks'—science lesson.

'Scally'—rough, untidy boy.

'Stand'—platform on which chief and second chief petty officers beds stood.

'Sea draft'—boys in their last six months at the school; at one time this period would have been spent living on board the 'ship'.

'Tiddy or Tiddley Oggies'—Cornish pasties, issued on leave mornings to those travelling long distances.

'Tallies'—pieces of canvas sewn on to each sock bearing company letter and number.

'Tar's bow'—fancy bow tied in cap ribbon.

'Trim up'—civilian haircut.

'Togger, Tog'—smoker, to smoke.

'Toke'—bread.

'Torch'—beef dripping.

'Tuskies, Tusker'—teeth; boy with large teeth.

'Tiddley'—neat.

'Tabs'—see Tallies.

'Walking Sunday'—Sunday before leave.

'Whack'—portion.

'Wet shirt'—hard task, unpleasant job.

'Whistlers'—eggs.

'Wipe back'—drying up water with a deck-cloth, especially walking back dragging the cloth from side to side with both hands.

THE DEPARTURE

I have looked from my window
And watched the Boys
   In drill slips and busy at play.
All laughing and merry and all in a hurry,
   For time passes away.

I have looked from my window,
The gym, flagged so gay.
The Boy's friends—Their Day.
For dancing and hornpipe, marching and drill,
   A display they all like to see.

I look from my window,
   Boys shouting and fighting with glee.
For a fight is a sight.
   For fair play to back,
They laugh and they shout
   Till the lockers they crack.

I look from my window,
The same boys are there, Faces are eager again
For bread and cheese are there to please,
A portion for each boy to share.
Or biscuit or cake, but not Mum's Make.*

I look from my window and see the Boys
In a hundred of different ways,
But the way I'll remember to the end of my days,
   Are the hymns that they sung
   And the motto that hung,
Fear God and honour the King.

I look from my window,
Boys line up to pray. The silence one feels
As we murmur Amen. And you feel that each lad
Has a Mum or a Dad who will be proud of the man some day.

I look from my window
For the last time once more,
Not a boy shall I see there again.
There shouting and laughing, marching and
All in a hurry.
For time has all passed away.

> Mrs. Amberley.
> From the Tuck-shop window.

*The cake was, in fact, currant bread served for supper.

LIST OF PRINCIPALS AND SUPERINTENDENTS*

1716	Thomas Weston, Headmaster (Weston's Academy).
1747	Burney's Academy (Mr. Burney Principal?)†
1758	New School.
1788–1821	Charles Burney, Headmaster.
18–	Reverend Turrot. Relieved by
18–	Mr. W. Boyd. Superseded by
1821	Mr. Edward Riddle. Followed by his son
1851	Mr. John Riddle.
1856–1863	Reverend Fisher, Headmaster.
1856–1863	Lieutenant Rouse, Superintendent.**
1867	Reverend Holmes.
1870–1878	Captain Charles Burney, Superintendent.
—	Captain W. V. Anson, Superintendent.
1898	Commander George Huntingford, Superintendent.
1906	Captain E. M. Cooper-Key, C.B., M.V.O., R.N. (Ret.), Superintendent.
1922	Captain, later Rear Admiral L. R. Oliphant, R.N. (Ret.), Superintendent.
1932	Captain E. Bruce-Gardyne, D.S.O., R.N., Superintendent.

*This list may be incomplete as to dates and perhaps a few other details but appears to be all the information available at this time.

†When the new school was completed in 1758, Burney's Academy continued at the same premises until 1782 when the school moved to a house at the foot of Crooms Hill, on the site once occupied by the mansion called 'Audley House'; about six years later it was taken over by Fanny Burney's brother, Charles, and run by himself and his son, Dr. Charles Parr Burney, for nearly forty years until the whole establishment moved to Portsmouth about 1825.

**It appears that Lieutenant Rouse was the first Superintendent, and as such served during the periods when the Reverends Fisher and Holmes were headmasters.

SCHOOL STAFF 1929

Superintendent   Rear Admiral L. R. Oliphant, R.N. (Ret.).
Cashier   Paymaster-Captain B. W. G. Cook, O.B.E., R.N. (Ret.).
Medical Officer   Surgeon-Captain P. M. May, R.N. (Ret.).
Chaplain   Reverend A. D. Gilbertson, M.A., R.N.
Chief Officer   Lieutenant-Commander S. T. P. Yeo, R.N. (Ret.).
Assistant Chaplain   Reverend G. I. Soden, B.A.

EDUCATIONAL STAFF

Headmaster   Mr. S. R. Hewitson, B.Sc., F.R.A.S.
Divisional Masters   Mr. E. E. Perrin, M.Sc., Upper Nautical.
    Mr. H. T. Arnold, Senior Division.
    Mr. A. E. Sheldrake, Junior Division.

Masters

Upper Nautical	Senior Division	Junior Division
Mr. M. Morling	Mr. A. F. Timmis	Mr. F. C. Cowell
Mr. A. Ward	Mr. W. H. Pine	Mr. W. W. Caseley
Mr. T. A. Lumsden	Mr. F. G. Wallington	Mr. B. J. Evans
Mr. N. Hurst	Mr. N. S. Arness	Mr. J. E. Rice
	Mr. J. Coyle	Mr. W. Blackman
Science Dept.	Mr. W. H. Wood	Mr. G. A. Hewitt
	Mr. E. A. Snee	Mr. C. J. Long
Mr. S. T. Barker		Mr. F. J. Buckley
		Mr. E. A. Jones
		Mr. W. A. Smith

Company Officers

No. 1 Mr. F. Coombes   Mr. F. W. Abberley (dining-hall)
No. 2 Mr. W. A. Cressey   Mr. W. J. Simmons (gate and post office)
No. 3 Mr. R. J. Smith   Mr. G. Ray (Trafalgar quarters)
No. 4 Mr. F. Storey   Mr. P. Wilson (B company)

No. 5 Mr. H. Faulkner   Mr. W. J. Searles
No. 6 Mr. G. Wyatt   Mr. E. Dimmock
No. 7 Mr. W. G. Bushnell
No. 8 Mr. H. O. Dickenson   *Bandmaster*
No. 9 Mr. S. L. Evans   Mr. J. S. Brown

Active Service Ratings

P.O. A. C. Gregory, P. and R.T.I.   L.S. G. L. French, P. and R.T.I.
P.O. A. C. Clisby, P. and R.T.I.   L.S. R. W. Burton, P. and R.T.I.
      Acting-Corporal R. M., A. E. Swift, Band Corporal.

INDEX